I0154733

FOREWORD

The collection of "Everything Will Be Okay" travel phrasebooks published by T&P Books is designed for people traveling abroad for tourism and business. The phrasebooks contain what matters most - the essentials for basic communication. This is an indispensable set of phrases to "survive" while abroad.

This phrasebook will help you in most cases where you need to ask something, get directions, find out how much something costs, etc. It can also resolve difficult communication situations where gestures just won't help.

This book contains a lot of phrases that have been grouped according to the most relevant topics. The edition also includes a small vocabulary that contains roughly 3,000 of the most frequently used words. Another section of the phrasebook provides a gastronomical dictionary that may help you order food at a restaurant or buy groceries at the store.

Take "Everything Will Be Okay" phrasebook with you on the road and you'll have an irreplaceable traveling companion who will help you find your way out of any situation and teach you to not fear speaking with foreigners.

TABLE OF CONTENTS

T&P Books Publishing

Travel phrasebooks collection
«Everything Will Be Okay!»

T&P Books Publishing

PHRASEBOOK

ARABIC

By Andrey Taranov

THE MOST IMPORTANT PHRASES

This phrasebook contains the most important phrases and questions for basic communication Everything you need to survive overseas

T&P BOOKS

Phrasebook + 3000-word dictionary

English-Egyptian Arabic phrasebook & topical vocabulary

By Andrey Taranov

The collection of "Everything Will Be Okay" travel phrasebooks published by T&P Books is designed for people traveling abroad for tourism and business. The phrasebooks contain what matters most - the essentials for basic communication. This is an indispensable set of phrases to "survive" while abroad.

This book also includes a small topical vocabulary that contains roughly 3,000 of the most frequently used words. Another section of the phrasebook provides a gastronomical dictionary that may help you order food at a restaurant or buy groceries at the store.

T&P Books Publishing
www.tpbooks.com

ISBN: 978-1-78716-931-9

This book is also available in E-book formats.
Please visit www.tpbooks.com or the major online bookstores.

PRONUNCIATION

T&P phonetic alphabet	Egyptian Arabic example	English example
[a]	[ṭaffa] طفّى	shorter than in ask
[ā]	[eχtār] إختار	calf, palm
[e]	[setta] ستّة	elm, medal
[i]	[minā'] ميناء	shorter than in feet
[ī]	[ebrīl] إبريل	feet, meter
[o]	[oɣosṭos] أغسطس	pod, John
[ō]	[ḥalazōn] حلزون	fall, bomb
[u]	[kalkutta] كلكتا	book
[ū]	[gamūs] جاموس	fuel, tuna
[b]	[bedāya] بداية	baby, book
[d]	[sa'āda] سعادة	day, doctor
[ḍ]	[waḍ'] وضع	[d] pharyngeal
[ʒ]	[arʒantīn] الأرجنتين	forge, pleasure
[ẓ]	[ẓahar] ظهر	[z] pharyngeal
[f]	[χafīf] خفيف	face, food
[g]	[bahga] بهجة	game, gold
[h]	[ettegāh] إتّجاه	home, have
[ḥ]	[ḥabb] حبّ	[h] pharyngeal
[y]	[dahaby] ذهبي	yes, New York
[k]	[korsy] كرسي	clock, kiss
[l]	[lammaḥ] لمّح	lace, people
[m]	[marṣad] مرصد	magic, milk
[n]	[ganūb] جنوب	sang, thing
[p]	[kaputʃino] كابتشينو	pencil, private
[q]	[wasaq] وثق	king, club
[r]	[roḥe] روح	rice, radio
[s]	[soχreya] سخرية	city, boss
[ṣ]	[me'ṣam] معصم	[s] pharyngeal
[ʃ]	['aʃā'] عشاء	machine, shark
[t]	[tanūb] تنوب	tourist, trip
[ṭ]	[χarīṭa] خريطة	[t] pharyngeal
[θ]	[mamūθ] ماموث	month, tooth
[v]	[vietnām] فيتنام	very, river
[w]	[wadda'] ودّع	vase, winter
[χ]	[baχīl] بخيل	as in Scots 'loch'
[ɣ]	[etɣadda] إتغدّى	between [g] and [h]

T&P phonetic alphabet	Egyptian Arabic example	English example
[z]	[me'za] معزة	zebra, please
['] (ayn)	[sab'a] سبعة	voiced pharyngeal fricative
['] (hamza)	[sa'al] سأل	glottal stop

LIST OF ABBREVIATIONS

Egyptian Arabic abbreviations

du	-	plural noun (double)
f	-	feminine noun
m	-	masculine noun
pl	-	plural

English abbreviations

ab.	-	about
adj	-	adjective
adv	-	adverb
anim.	-	animate
as adj	-	attributive noun used as adjective
e.g.	-	for example
etc.	-	et cetera
fam.	-	familiar
fem.	-	feminine
form.	-	formal
inanim.	-	inanimate
masc.	-	masculine
math	-	mathematics
mil.	-	military
n	-	noun
pl	-	plural
pron.	-	pronoun
sb	-	somebody
sing.	-	singular
sth	-	something
v aux	-	auxiliary verb
vi	-	intransitive verb
vi, vt	-	intransitive, transitive verb
vt	-	transitive verb

ARABIC PHRASEBOOK

This section contains important phrases that may come in handy in various real-life situations.
The phrasebook will help you ask for directions, clarify a price, buy tickets, and order food at a restaurant

T&P Books Publishing

PHRASEBOOK CONTENTS

T&P Books Publishing

The bare minimum

Excuse me, …	law samaḥt, …	لو سمحت، …
Hello.	as salāmu ʿalaykum	السلام عليكم
Thank you.	ʃukran	شكرا
Good bye.	maʿ as salāma	مع السلامة
Yes.	naʿam	نعم
No.	la	لا
I don't know.	la aʿrif	لا أعرف
Where? | Where to? | When?	ayna? | ila ayna? | mata?	أين؟ | إلى أين؟ | متى؟

I need …	ana aḥtāʒ ila ...	أنا أحتاج إلى...
I want …	ana urīd …	أنا أريد …
Do you have …?	hal ʿindak …?	هل عندك… ؟
Is there a … here?	hal yūʒad huna …?	هل يوجد هنا …؟
May I …?	hal yumkinuni …?	هل يمكنني…؟
…, please (polite request)	… min faḍlak	من فضلك …

I'm looking for …	abḥaθ ʿan ...	أبحث عن …
restroom	ḥammām	حمام
ATM	mākīnat ṣarrāf ʾāliy	ماكينة صراف آلي
pharmacy (drugstore)	ṣaydaliyya	صيدلية
hospital	mustaʃfa	مستشفى
police station	qism aʃ ʃurṭa	قسم شرطة
subway	mitru al anfāq	مترو الأنفاق

taxi	taksi تاكسي
train station	mahattat al qiṭār محطة القطار

My name is ...	ismi ... إسمي...
What's your name?	ma smuka? ما اسمك؟
Could you please help me?	sāʿidni min faḍlak ساعدني من فضلك
I've got a problem.	ʿindi muʃkila عندي مشكلة
I don't feel well.	la aʃur bi χayr لا أشعر بخير
Call an ambulance!	ittaṣil bil isʿāf! إتصل بالإسعاف!
May I make a call?	hal yumkinuni iʒrāʾ mukālama tilifūniyya? هل يمكنني إجراء مكالمة هاتفية؟

I'm sorry.	ana ʾāṣif أنا آسف
You're welcome.	al ʿafw العفو

I, me	ana أنا
you (inform.)	anta أنت
he	huwa هو
she	hiya هي
they (masc.)	hum هم
they (fem.)	hum هم
we	nahnu نحن
you (pl)	antum أنتم
you (sg, form.)	ḥaḍritak حضرتك

ENTRANCE	duχūl دخول
EXIT	χurūʒ خروج
OUT OF ORDER	muʿattal معطل
CLOSED	muɣlaq مغلق

OPEN	maftūḥ **مفتوح**
FOR WOMEN	lis sayyidāt **للسيدات**
FOR MEN	lir riʒāl **للرجال**

Questions

Where?	ayna? أين؟
Where to?	ila ayna? إلى أين؟
Where from?	min ayna? من أين؟
Why?	limāða? لماذا؟
For what reason?	li ayy sabab? لأي سبب؟
When?	mata? متى؟
How long?	kam waqt? كم وقتا؟
At what time?	fi ayy sā'a? في أي ساعة؟
How much?	bikam? بكم؟
Do you have ...?	hal 'indak ...? هل عندك ...؟
Where is ...?	ayna ...? أين ...؟
What time is it?	as sā'a kam? الساعة كم؟
May I make a call?	hal yumkinuni iʒrā' mukālama tilifūniyya? هل يمكنني إجراء مكالمة هاتفية؟
Who's there?	man hunāk? من هناك؟
Can I smoke here?	hal yumkinuni at tadχīn huna? هل يمكنني التدخين هنا؟
May I ...?	hal yumkinuni ...? هل يمكنني ...؟

Needs

I'd like ...	urīd an ... **أريد أن...**
I don't want ...	la urīd an ... **لا أريد أن...**
I'm thirsty.	ana ʿatʃān **أنا عطشان**
I want to sleep.	urīd an anām **أريد أن أنام**
I want ...	urīd an ... **أريد أن...**
to wash up	aɣtasil **أغتسل**
to brush my teeth	unazzif asnāni **أنظف أسناني**
to rest a while	astarīḥ qalīlan **أستريح قليلا**
to change my clothes	uɣayyir malābisi **أغير ملابسي**
to go back to the hotel	arʒiʿ ilal funduq **أرجع إلى الفندق**
to buy ...	aʃtari ... **أشتري ...**
to go to ...	aðhab ila ... **أذهب إلى ...**
to visit ...	azūr ... **أزور ...**
to meet with ...	uqābil ... **أقابل ...**
to make a call	uʒri mukālama hātifiyya **أجري مكالمة هاتفية**
I'm tired.	ana taʿibt **أنا تعبت**
We are tired.	naḥnu taʿibna **نحن تعبنا**
I'm cold.	ana bardān **أنا بردان**
I'm hot.	ana ḥarrān **أنا حران**
I'm OK.	ana bi χayr **أنا بخير**

I need to make a call.	aḥtāʒ ila iʒrā' mukālama hātifiyya **أحتاج إلى إجراء مكالمة هاتفية**
I need to go to the restroom.	aḥtāʒ ila ḥammām **أحتاج إلى حمام**
I have to go.	yaʒib 'alayya an aðhab **يجب علي أن أذهب**
I have to go now.	yaʒib 'alayya an aðhab al 'ān **يجب علي أن أذهب الآن**

Asking for directions

Excuse me, ...	law samaḥt, ... **لو سمحت، ...**
Where is ...?	ayna ...? **أين ...؟**
Which way is ...?	ayna aṭ ṭarīq ila ...? **أين الطريق إلى ...؟**
Could you help me, please?	hal yumkinak musā'adati, min faḍlak? **هل يمكنك مساعدتي، من فضلك؟**
I'm looking for ...	abḥaθ 'an ... **أبحث عن ...**
I'm looking for the exit.	abḥaθ 'an ṭarīq al χurūʒ **أبحث عن طريق الخروج**
I'm going to ...	ana ðāhib ila... **أنا ذاهب إلى...**
Am I going the right way to ...?	hal ana 'alaṭ ṭarīq as ṣaḥīḥ ila ...? **هل أنا على الطريق الصحيح إلى... ؟**
Is it far?	hal huwa ba'īd? **هل هو بعيد؟**
Can I get there on foot?	hal yumkinuni an aṣil ila hunāk māʃiyan? **هل يمكنني أن أصل إلى هناك ماشيا؟**
Can you show me on the map?	arīni 'alal χarīṭa min faḍlak **أريني على الخريطة من فضلك**
Show me where we are right now.	arīni naḥnu ayna al 'ān **أريني أين نحن الآن**
Here	huna **هنا**
There	hunāk **هناك**
This way	min huna **من هنا**
Turn right.	in'aṭif yamīnan **إنعطف يمينا**
Turn left.	in'aṭif yasāran **إنعطف يسارا**
first (second, third) turn	awwal (θāni, θāliθ) ʃāri' **أول (ثاني، ثالث) شارع**

to the right	ilal yamīn **إلى اليمين**
to the left	ilal yasār **إلى اليسار**
Go straight ahead.	iðhab ilal amām mubāʃaratan **إذهب إلى أمام مباشرة**

Signs

WELCOME!	marḥaban	مرحبا
ENTRANCE	duχūl	دخول
EXIT	χurūʒ	خروج
PUSH	idfa'	إدفع
PULL	isḥab	إسحب
OPEN	maftūḥ	مفتوح
CLOSED	muɣlaq	مغلق
FOR WOMEN	lis sayyidāt	للسيدات
FOR MEN	lir riʒāl	للرجال
GENTLEMEN, GENTS (m)	ar riʒāl	الرجال
WOMEN (f)	as sayyidāt	السيدات
DISCOUNTS	taχfīḍāt	تخفيضات
SALE	'ūkazyūn	أوكازيون
FREE	maʒʒānan	مجانا
NEW!	ʒadīd!	جديد!
ATTENTION!	intabih!	إنتبه!
NO VACANCIES	la tūʒad ɣuraf χāliya	لا توجد غرف خالية
RESERVED	maḥʒūz	محجوز
ADMINISTRATION	al idāra	الإدارة
STAFF ONLY	lil 'āmilīn faqaṭ	للعاملين فقط

BEWARE OF THE DOG!	iḥtaris min al kalb! إحترس من الكلب!
NO SMOKING!	mamnūʿ at tadχīn! ممنوع التدخين!
DO NOT TOUCH!	mamnūʿ al lams! ممنوع اللمس!
DANGEROUS	χaṭīr خطير
DANGER	χaṭar خطر
HIGH VOLTAGE	ʒuhd ʿāli جهد عالي
NO SWIMMING!	mamnūʿ as sibāḥa! ممنوع السباحة!

OUT OF ORDER	muʿaṭṭal معطل
FLAMMABLE	qābil lil iʃtiʿāl قابل للإشتعال
FORBIDDEN	mamnūʿ ممنوع
NO TRESPASSING!	mamnūʿ at taʿaddi! ممنوع التعدي!
WET PAINT	ṭilāʾ ḥadīθ طلاء حديث

CLOSED FOR RENOVATIONS	muɣlaq lit taʒdīdāt مغلق للتجديدات
WORKS AHEAD	amāmak aʿmāl fiṭ ṭarīq أمامك أعمال طرق
DETOUR	taḥwīla تحويلة

Transportation. General phrases

plane	ṭā'ira **طائرة**
train	qiṭār **قطار**
bus	ḥāfila **حافلة**
ferry	safīna **سفينة**
taxi	taksi **تاكسي**
car	sayyāra **سيارة**

schedule	ʒadwal **جدول**
Where can I see the schedule?	ayna yumkinuni an ara al ʒadwal? **أين يمكنني أن أرى الجدول؟**
workdays (weekdays)	ayyām al usbū' **أيام الأسبوع**
weekends	nihāyat al usbū' **نهاية الأسبوع**
holidays	ayyām al 'uṭla ar rasmiyya **أيام العطلة الرسمية**

DEPARTURE	al muɣādara **المغادرة**
ARRIVAL	al wuṣūl **الوصول**
DELAYED	muta'aχχira **متأخرة**
CANCELLED	ulɣiyat **ألغيت**

next (train, etc.)	al qādim **القادم**
first	al awwal **الأول**
last	al aχīr **الأخير**

When is the next ...?	mata al ... al qādim? **القادم؟ ... متى الـ**
When is the first ...?	mata awwal ...? **متى أول ...؟**

When is the last ...?	mata 'āχir ...? **متى آخر ...؟**
transfer (change of trains, etc.)	taɣyīr **تغيير**
to make a transfer	uɣayyir **أغير**
Do I need to make a transfer?	hal yaʒib 'alayya taɣyīr al ...? **هل يجب علي تغيير الـ...؟**

Buying tickets

Where can I buy tickets?	ayna yumkinuni ʃirā' tazākir? أين يمكنني شراء التذاكر؟
ticket	taðkara تذكرة
to buy a ticket	ʃirā' at taðkira شراء تذكرة
ticket price	si'r at taðkira سعر التذكرة

Where to?	ila ayna? إلى أين؟
To what station?	ila ayy maḥaṭṭa? إلى أي محطة؟
I need …	ana urīd … أنا أريد …
one ticket	taðkara wāḥida تذكرة واحدة
two tickets	taðkaratayn تذكرتين
three tickets	θalāθat taðākir ثلاث تذاكر

one-way	ðahāb faqaṭ ذهاب فقط
round-trip	ðahāban wa iyāban ذهابا وإيابا
first class	ad daraʒa al ūla الدرجة الأولى
second class	ad daraʒa aθ θāniya الدرجة الثانية

today	al yawm اليوم
tomorrow	ɣadan غدا
the day after tomorrow	ba'd ɣad بعد غد
in the morning	fiṣ ṣabāḥ في الصباح
in the afternoon	ba'd aẓ ẓuhr بعد الظهر
in the evening	fil masā' في المساء

aisle seat	maqʿad bi ʒānib al mamarr **مقعد بجانب الممر**
window seat	maqʿad bi ʒānib an nāfiða **مقعد بجانب النافذة**
How much?	bikam? **بكم؟**
Can I pay by credit card?	hal yumkinuni an adfaʿ bi biṭāqat iʾtimān? **هل يمكنني أن أدفع ببطاقة إئتمان؟**

Bus

bus	ḥāfila حافلة
intercity bus	ḥāfila bayn al mudun حافلة بين المدن
bus stop	maḥaṭṭat al ḥāfilāt محطة الحافلات
Where's the nearest bus stop?	ayna aqrab maḥaṭṭat al ḥāfilāt? أين أقرب محطة الحافلات؟
number (bus ~, etc.)	raqm رقم
Which bus do I take to get to ...?	ayy ḥāfila ta'χuðuni ila ...? أي حافلة تأخذني إلى...؟
Does this bus go to ...?	hal taðhab haðihil ḥāfila ila ...? هل تذهب هذه الحافلة إلى...؟
How frequent are the buses?	kam marra taðhab al ḥāfilāt? كم مرة تذهب الحافلات؟
every 15 minutes	kull χams ʿaʃara daqīqa كل 15 دقيقة
every half hour	kull niṣf sāʿa كل نصف ساعة
every hour	kull sāʿa كل ساعة
several times a day	ʿiddat marrāt fil yawm عدة مرات في اليوم
... times a day	... marrāt fil yawm ... مرات في اليوم
schedule	ʒadwal جدول
Where can I see the schedule?	ayna yumkinuni an ara al ʒadwal? أين يمكنني أن أرى الجدول؟
When is the next bus?	mata al ḥāfila al qādima? متى الحافلة القادمة؟
When is the first bus?	mata awwal ḥāfila? متى أول حافلة؟
When is the last bus?	mata 'āχir ḥāfila? متى آخر حافلة؟
stop	maḥaṭṭa محطة
next stop	al maḥaṭṭa al qādima المحطة القادمة

last stop (terminus)	āχir maḥaṭṭa **آخر محطة**
Stop here, please.	qif huna min faḍlak **قف هنا من فضلك**
Excuse me, this is my stop.	law samaḥt, haðihi maḥaṭṭati **لو سمحت، هذه محطتي**

Train

train	qiṭār قطار
suburban train	qiṭār aḍ ḍawāḥi قطار الضواحي
long-distance train	qiṭār al masāfāt aṭ ṭawīla قطار المسافات الطويلة
train station	maḥaṭṭat al qiṭārāt محطة القطارات
Excuse me, where is the exit to the platform?	law samaḥt, ayna aṭ ṭarīq ilar raṣīf لو سمحت، أين الطريق إلى الرصيف؟
Does this train go to ...?	ha yatawaʒʒah haðal qiṭār ila ...? هل يتوجه هذا القطار إلى ...؟
next train	al qiṭār al qādim القطار القادم
When is the next train?	mata al qiṭār al qādim? متى القطار القادم؟
Where can I see the schedule?	ayna yumkinuni an ara al ʒadwal? أين يمكنني أن أرى الجدول؟
From which platform?	min ayy raṣīf? من أي رصيف؟
When does the train arrive in ...?	mata yaṣil al qiṭār ila ...? متى يصل القطار إلى... ؟
Please help me.	sāʿidni min faḍlak ساعدني من فضلك
I'm looking for my seat.	ana abḥaθ ʿan maqʿadi أنا أبحث عن مقعدي
We're looking for our seats.	naḥnu nabḥaθ ʿan maqāʿidina نحن نبحث عن مقاعدنا
My seat is taken.	maqʿadi maʃɣūl مقعدي مشغول
Our seats are taken.	maqāʿiduna maʃɣūla مقاعدنا مشغولة
I'm sorry but this is my seat.	ana ʾāsif lakin haða maqʿadi أنا آسف، ولكن هذا مقعدي
Is this seat taken?	hal haðal maqʿad maḥʒūz? هل هذا المقعد محجوز؟
May I sit here?	hal yumkinuni an aqʿud huna? هل يمكنني أن أقعد هنا؟

On the train. Dialogue (No ticket)

Ticket, please.	taðākir min faḍlak تذاكر من فضلك
I don't have a ticket.	laysat 'indi taðkira ليست عندي تذكرة
I lost my ticket.	taðkarati ḍā'at تذكرتي ضاعت
I forgot my ticket at home.	nasīt taðkirati fil bayt نسيت تذكرتي في البيت
You can buy a ticket from me.	yumkinak an taʃtari minni taðkira يمكنك أن تشتري مني تذكرة
You will also have to pay a fine.	kama yaʒib 'alayk an tadfa' ɣarāma كما يجب عليك أن تدفع غرامة
Okay.	ḥasanan حسنا
Where are you going?	ila ayna taðhab? إلى أين تذهب؟
I'm going to ...	aðhab ila ... أذهب إلى ...
How much? I don't understand.	bikam? ana la afham بكم؟ أنا لا أفهم
Write it down, please.	uktubha min faḍlak إكتبها من فضلك
Okay. Can I pay with a credit card?	ḥasanan. hal yumkinuni an adfa' bi biṭāqat i'timān? حسنا. هل يمكنني أن أدفع ببطاقة إئتمان؟
Yes, you can.	na'am yumkinuk نعم يمكنك
Here's your receipt.	tafaḍḍal al 'īṣāl تفضل الإيصال
Sorry about the fine.	'āsif bi χuṣūṣ al ɣarāma أنا آسف بخصوص الغرامة
That's okay. It was my fault.	laysa hunāk ayy muʃkila. haðihi ɣalṭati ليس هناك أي مشكلة. هذه غلطتي
Enjoy your trip.	istamta' bi riḥlatak إستمتع برحلتك

Taxi

taxi	taksi **تاكسي**
taxi driver	sā'iq at taksi **سائق التاكسي**
to catch a taxi	'āχuð taksi **أخذ تاكسي**
taxi stand	mawqif taksi **موقف تاكسي**
Where can I get a taxi?	ayna yumkinuni an 'āχuð taksi? **أين يمكنني أن آخذ تاكسي؟**

---

to call a taxi	ṭalab taksi **طلب تاكسي**
I need a taxi.	aḥtāʒ ila taksi **أحتاج إلى تاكسي**
Right now.	al 'ān **الآن**
What is your address (location)?	ma huwa ʿunwānak? **ما هو عنوانك؟**
My address is ...	ʿunwāni fi ... **عنواني في ...**
Your destination?	ila ayna taðhab? **إلى أين تذهب؟**
Excuse me, ...	law samaḥt, ... **لو سمحت، ...**
Are you available?	hal anta fādy? **هل أنت فاض؟**
How much is it to get to ...?	kam adfaʿ li aṣil ila ...? **كم أدفع لأصل إلى...؟**
Do you know where it is?	hal taʿrif ayna hiya? **هل تعرف أين هي؟**

Airport, please.	ilal maṭār min faḍlak **إلى المطار من فضلك**
Stop here, please.	qif huna min faḍlak **قف هنا، من فضلك**
It's not here.	innaha laysat huna **إنها ليست هنا**
This is the wrong address.	al ʿunwān χāṭi' **العنوان خاطئ**
Turn left.	inʿaṭif ilal yasār **إنعطف إلى اليسار**
Turn right.	inʿaṭif ilal yamīn **إنعطف إلى اليمين**

How much do I owe you?	kam ana mudīn lak? كم أنا مدين لك؟
I'd like a receipt, please.	aʿṭini ʾīṣāl min faḍlak. أعطني إيصالا، من فضلك.
Keep the change.	iḥtafiẓ bil bāqi إحتفظ بالباقي

Would you please wait for me?	intaẓirni min faḍlak إنتظرني من فضلك
five minutes	χams daqāʾiq خمس دقائق
ten minutes	ʿaʃar daqāʾiq عشر دقائق
fifteen minutes	rubʿ sāʿa ربع ساعة
twenty minutes	θulθ sāʿa ثلث ساعة
half an hour	niṣf sāʿa نصف ساعة

Hotel

Hello.	as salāmu ʻalaykum **السلام عليكم**
My name is ...	ismi ... **إسمي ...**
I have a reservation.	ʻindi ḥaʒz **لدي حجز**
I need ...	urīd ... **أريد ...**
a single room	ɣurfa li ʃaχṣ wāḥid **غرفة لشخص واحد**
a double room	ɣurfa li ʃaχṣayn **غرفة لشخصين**
How much is that?	kam siʻruha? **كم سعرها؟**
That's a bit expensive.	hiya ɣāliya **هي غالية**
Do you have anything else?	hal ʻindak χiyārāt uχra? **هل عندك خيارات أخرى؟**
I'll take it.	āχuðuha **آخذها**
I'll pay in cash.	adfaʻ naqdan **أدفع نقدا**
I've got a problem.	ʻindi muʃkila **عندي مشكلة**
My ... is broken.	... muʻaṭṭal **... معطل**
My ... is out of order.	... muʻaṭṭal /muʻaṭṭala/ **.../معطل /معطلة**
TV	at tilivizyūn **التليفزيون**
air conditioner	at takyīf **التكييف**
tap	al ḥanafiyya **الحنفية**
shower	ad duʃ **الدوش**
sink	al ḥawḍ **الحوض**
safe	al χazīna **الخزينة**

door lock	qifl al bāb **قفل الباب**
electrical outlet	maχraʒ al kahrabā' **مخرج الكهرباء**
hairdryer	muʒaffif aʃ ʃa'r **مجفف الشعر**

I don't have ...	laysa ladayya ... **ليس لدي ...**
water	mā' **ماء**
light	nūr **نور**
electricity	kahrabā' **كهرباء**

Can you give me ...?	hal yumkinak an ta'ṭīni ...? **هل يمكنك أن تعطيني ...؟**
a towel	fūṭa **فوطة**
a blanket	baṭṭāniyya **بطانية**
slippers	ʃabāʃib **شباشب**
a robe	rūb **روب**
shampoo	ʃambu **شامبو**
soap	ṣābūn **صابون**

I'd like to change rooms.	urīd an uɣayyir al ɣurfa **أريد أن أغير الغرفة**
I can't find my key.	la astaṭī' an aʒid miftāḥi **لا أستطيع أن أجد مفتاحي**
Could you open my room, please?	iftaḥ ɣurfati min faḍlak **إفتح غرفتي من فضلك**
Who's there?	man hunāk? **من هناك؟**
Come in!	tafaḍḍal! **تفضل!**
Just a minute!	daqīqa wāḥida! **دقيقة واحدة!**
Not right now, please.	laysa al 'ān min faḍlak **ليس الآن من فضلك**

Come to my room, please.	ta'āla ila ɣurfati law samaḥt **تعال إلى غرفتي لو سمحت**
I'd like to order food service.	urīd an yuḥḍar aṭ ṭa'ām ila ɣurfati **أريد أن يحضر الطعام إلى غرفتي**
My room number is ...	raqm gurfati huwa ... **رقم غرفتي هو ...**

I'm leaving ...	uɣādir ... **أغادر ...**
We're leaving ...	nuɣādir ... **نغادر ...**
right now	al ʾān **الآن**
this afternoon	baʿd aẓ ẓuhr **بعد الظهر**
tonight	masāʾ al yawm **مساء اليوم**
tomorrow	ɣadan **غداً**
tomorrow morning	ṣabāḥ al ɣad **صباح الغد**
tomorrow evening	masāʾ al ɣad **مساء الغد**
the day after tomorrow	baʿd ɣad **بعد غد**

I'd like to pay.	urīd an adfaʿ **أريد أن أدفع**
Everything was wonderful.	kull ʃayʾ kān rāʾiʿ **كل شيء كان رائعا**
Where can I get a taxi?	ayna yumkinuni an ʾāxuð taksi? **أين يمكنني أن آخذ تاكسي؟**
Would you call a taxi for me, please?	hal yumkinak an taṭlub li taksi law samaḥt? **هل يمكنك أن تطلب لي تاكسي لو سمحت؟**

Restaurant

Can I look at the menu, please?	hal yumkinuni an ara qā'imat aṭ ṭa'ām min faḍlak? هل يمكنني أن أرى قائمة الطعام من فضلك؟
Table for one.	mā'ida li ʃaχṣ wāḥid مائدة لشخص واحد
There are two (three, four) of us.	naḥnu iθnān (θalāθa, arba'a) نحن إثنان (ثلاثة، أربعة)
Smoking	lil mudaχχinīn للمدخنين
No smoking	li ɣayr al mudaχχinīn لغير المدخنين
Excuse me! (addressing a waiter)	law samaḥt لو سمحت
menu	qā'imat aṭ ṭa'ām قائمة الطعام
wine list	qā'imat an nabīð قائمة النبيذ
The menu, please.	al qā'ima, law samaḥt القائمة، لو سمحت
Are you ready to order?	hal anta musta'idd liṭ ṭalab? هل أنت مستعد للطلب؟
What will you have?	māða tā'χuð? ماذا تأخذ؟
I'll have ...	ana 'āhχuð ... أنا آخذ ...
I'm a vegetarian.	ana nabātiy أنا نباتي
meat	laḥm لحم
fish	samak سمك
vegetables	χuḍār خضار
Do you have vegetarian dishes?	hal 'indak aṭbāq nabātiyya? هل عندك أطباق نباتية؟
I don't eat pork.	la 'ākul al χinzīr لا آكل لحم الخنزير
He /she/ doesn't eat meat.	huwa la ya'kul /hiya la ta'kul / al laḥm هو لا يأكل /هي لا تأكل/ اللحم

I am allergic to …	ʿindi ḥassāsiyya ḍidda … عندي حساسية ضد …
Would you please bring me …	aḥḍir li … min faḍlak أحضر لي... من فضلك
salt | pepper | sugar	milḥ | filfil | sukkar سكر | فلفل | ملح
coffee | tea | dessert	qahwa | ʃāy | ḥalwa حلوى | شاي | قهوة
water | sparkling | plain	miyāh | ɣāziyya | bidūn ɣāz بدون غاز | غازية | مياه
a spoon | fork | knife	milʿaqa | ʃawka | sikkīn سكين | شوكة | ملعقة
a plate | napkin	ṭabaq | fūṭa فوطة| طبق

Enjoy your meal!	bil hināʾ waʃ ʃifāʾ بالهناء والشفاء
One more, please.	wāḥida kamān law samaḥt واحدة كمان من فضلك
It was very delicious.	kānat laðīða giddan كانت لذيذة جدا

---

check | change | tip	ḥisāb | fakka | baqʃīʃ بقشيش| فكة| حساب
Check, please. (Could I have the check, please?)	aḥḍir li al ḥisāb min faḍlak? أحضر لي الحساب من فضلك
Can I pay by credit card?	hal yumkinuni an adfaʿ bi biṭāqat iʾtimān? هل يمكنني أن أدفع ببطاقة إئتمان؟
I'm sorry, there's a mistake here.	ana ʾāsif, hunāk xaṭaʾ أنا آسف، هناك خطأ

Shopping

Can I help you?	momken usāʿidak? هل أستطيع أن أساعدك؟
Do you have ...?	hal ʿindak ...? هل عندك ...؟
I'm looking for ...	ana abḥaθ ʿan ... أنا أبحث عن ...
I need ...	urīd ... أريد ...
I'm just looking.	ana faqat anẓur أنا فقط أنظر
We're just looking.	naḥnu faqat nanẓur نحن فقط ننظر
I'll come back later.	saʾaʿūd lāḥiqan سأعود لاحقا
We'll come back later.	sanaʿūd lāḥiqan سنعود لاحقا
discounts | sale	taɣfīḍāt | ʾūkazyūn أوكازيون تخفيضات
Would you please show me ...	arīni ... min faḍlak أريني ... من فضلك
Would you please give me ...	aʿṭini ... min faḍlak أعطني ... من فضلك
Can I try it on?	hal yumkin an uʒarribahu? هل يمكن أن أجربه؟
Excuse me, where's the fitting room?	law samaḥt, ayna ɣurfat al qiyās? لو سمحت، أين غرفة القياس؟
Which color would you like?	ayy lawn turīd? أي لون تريد؟
size | length	maqās | ṭūl طول امقاس
How does it fit?	hal yunāsibak? هل يناسبك؟
How much is it?	bikam? بكم؟
That's too expensive.	haða ɣāli ʒiddan هذا غال جدا
I'll take it.	aʃtarīhi أشتريه
Excuse me, where do I pay?	ayna yumkinuni an adfaʿ law samaḥt? أين يمكنني أن أدفع لو سمحت؟

Will you pay in cash or credit card?	hal tadfa' naqdan aw bi biṭāqat i'timān? **هل تدفع نقدا أو ببطاقة إئتمان؟**
In cash | with credit card	naqdan | bi biṭāqat i'timān **ببطاقة إئتمان ا نقدا**

Do you want the receipt?	hal turīd īṣāl? **هل تريد إيصالا؟**
Yes, please.	na'am, min faḍlak **نعم، من فضلك**
No, it's OK.	la, laysa hunāk ayy moʃkila **لا، ليس هناك أي مشكلة**
Thank you. Have a nice day!	ʃukran. yawmak sa'īd **شكرا. يومك سعيد**

In town

Excuse me, please.	law samaḥt لو سمحت
I'm looking for ...	ana abḥaθ ʿan ... أنا أبحث عن ...
the subway	mitru al anfāq مترو الأنفاق
my hotel	funduqi فندقي
the movie theater	as sinima السينما
a taxi stand	mawqif taksi موقف تاكسي
an ATM	mākīnat ṣarrāf ʾāliy ماكينة صراف آلي
a foreign exchange office	maktab ṣarrāfa مكتب صرافة
an internet café	maqha intirnit مقهى انترنت
... street	ʃāriʿ... شارع ...
this place	haðal makān هذا المكان
Do you know where ... is?	hal taʿrif ayna ...? هل تعرف أين ...؟
Which street is this?	ma ism haðaʃ ʃāriʿ? ما اسم هذا الشارع؟
Show me where we are right now.	arīni naḥnu ayna al ʾān? أريني أين نحن الآن؟
Can I get there on foot?	hal yumkinuni an aṣil ila hunāk māʃiyan? هل يمكنني أن أصل إلى هناك ماشيا؟
Do you have a map of the city?	hal ʿindak χarīṭa lil madīna? هل عندك خريطة للمدينة؟
How much is a ticket to get in?	bikam taðkarat ad duχūl? بكم تذكرة الدخول؟
Can I take pictures here?	hal yumkinuni at taṣwīr huna? هل يمكنني التصوير هنا؟
Are you open?	hal ... maftūḥ? هل ... مفتوح؟

When do you open?	mata taftaḥūn? **متى تفتحون؟**
When do you close?	mata tuɣliqūn? **متى تغلقون؟**

Money

money	nuqūd **نقود**
cash	naqd **نقد**
paper money	ʿumla waraqiyya **عملة ورقية**
loose change	fakka **فكة**
check | change | tip	ḥisāb | fakka | baqʃiʃ **حساب| فكة| بقشيش**
credit card	bitāqat iʾtimān **بطاقة إئتمان**
wallet	maḥfaẓat nuqūd **محفظة نقود**
to buy	ʃirāʾ **شراء**
to pay	dafʿ **دفع**
fine	ɣarāma **غرامة**
free	maʒʒānan **مجانا**
Where can I buy …?	ayna yumkinuni ʃirāʾ …? **أين يمكنني شراء ...؟**
Is the bank open now?	hal al bank maftūḥ al ʾān? **هل البنك مفتوح الآن؟**
When does it open?	mata taftaḥ? **متى يفتح؟**
When does it close?	mata yuɣliq? **متى يغلق؟**
How much?	bikam? **بكم؟**
How much is this?	bikam haða? **بكم هذا؟**
That's too expensive.	haða ɣāli ʒiddan **هذا غال جدا**
Excuse me, where do I pay?	ayna yumkinuni an adfaʿ law samaḥt? **أين يمكنني أن أدفع لو سمحت؟**
Check, please.	al ḥisāb min faḍlak **الحساب من فضلك**

Can I pay by credit card?	hal yumkinuni an adfaʿ bi biṭāqat iʾtimān? **هل يمكنني أن أدفع ببطاقة إئتمان؟**
Is there an ATM here?	hal tūʒad huna mākīnat ṣarrāf ʾāliy? **هل توجد هنا ماكينة صراف آلي؟**
I'm looking for an ATM.	ana abḥaθ ʿan mākīnat ṣarrāf ʾāliy **أنا أبحث عن ماكينة صراف آلي**

I'm looking for a foreign exchange office.	ana abḥaθ ʿan maktab ṣarrāfa **أنا أبحث عن مكتب صرافة**
I'd like to change ...	urīd taɣyīr ... **أريد تغيير ...**
What is the exchange rate?	kam siʿr al ʿumla? **كم سعر العملة؟**
Do you need my passport?	hal taḥtāʒ ila ʒawāz safari? **هل تحتاج إلى جواز سفري؟**

Time

What time is it?	as sā'a kam? الساعة كم؟
When?	mata? متى؟
At what time?	fi ayy sā'a? في أي ساعة؟
now | later | after ...	al 'ān | fi waqt lāhiq | ba'd ... الآن | في وقت لاحق | بعد ...
one o'clock	as sā'a al wāḥida الساعة الواحدة
one fifteen	as sā'a al wāḥida wa ar rub' الساعة الواحدة والربع
one thirty	as sā'a al wāḥida wa an niṣf الساعة الواحدة والنصف
one forty-five	as sā'a aθ θāniya illa rub' الساعة الثانية إلا ربعا
one | two | three	al wāḥida | aθ θāniya | aθ θāliθa الثالثة | الثانية | الواحدة
four | five | six	ar rābi'a | al χāmisa | as sādisa السادسة | الخامسة | الرابعة
seven | eight | nine	as sābi'a | aθ θāmina | at tāsi'a التاسعة | الثامنة | السابعة
ten | eleven | twelve	al 'āʃira | al ḥādiya 'aʃara | aθ θāniya 'aʃara الثانية عشرة | الحادية عشرة | العاشرة
in ...	ba'd ... بعد ...
five minutes	χams daqā'iq خمس دقائق
ten minutes	'aʃar daqā'iq عشر دقائق
fifteen minutes	rub' sā'a ربع ساعة
twenty minutes	θulθ sā'a ثلث ساعة
half an hour	niṣf sā'a نصف ساعة
an hour	sā'a ساعة

in the morning	fiṣ ṣabāḥ **في الصباح**
early in the morning	fiṣ ṣabāḥ al bākir **في الصباح الباكر**
this morning	ṣabāḥ al yawm **صباح اليوم**
tomorrow morning	ṣabāḥ al ɣad **صباح الغد**
in the middle of the day	fi muntaṣif an nahār **في منتصف النهار**
in the afternoon	ba'd aẓ ẓuhr **بعد الظهر**
in the evening	fil masā' **في المساء**
tonight	masā' al yawm **مساء اليوم**
at night	bil layl **بالليل**
yesterday	ams **أمس**
today	al yawm **اليوم**
tomorrow	ɣadan **غداً**
the day after tomorrow	ba'd ɣad **بعد غد**
What day is it today?	fi ayy yawm naḥnu? **في أي يوم نحن؟**
It's …	naḥnu fi … **نحن في …**
Monday	al iθnayn **الإثنين**
Tuesday	aθ θulāθā' **الثلاثاء**
Wednesday	al 'arbi'ā' **الأربعاء**
Thursday	al χamīs **الخميس**
Friday	al ʒum'a **الجمعة**
Saturday	as sabt **السبت**
Sunday	al aḥad **الأحد**

Greetings. Introductions

Hello.	as salāmu ʻalaykum **السلام عليكم**
Pleased to meet you.	ana saʻīd ʒiddan bi liqā'ik **أنا سعيد جدا بلقائك**
Me too.	ana asʻad **أنا أسعد**
I'd like you to meet ...	awudd an uʻarrifak bi ... **أود أن أعرفك بـ ...**
Nice to meet you.	furṣa saʻīda **فرصة سعيدة**

How are you?	kayf ḥālak? **كيف حالك؟**
My name is ...	ismi ... **أسمي ...**
His name is ...	ismuhu ... **إسمه ...**
Her name is ...	ismuha ... **إسمها ...**
What's your name?	ma smuka? **ما اسمك؟**
What's his name?	ma smuhu? **ما اسمه؟**
What's her name?	ma smuha? **ما اسمها؟**

What's your last name?	ma huwa ism ʻā'ilatak? **ما هو إسم عائلتك؟**
You can call me ...	yumkinak an tunādīni bi... **يمكنك أن تناديني بـ...**
Where are you from?	min ayna anta? **من أين أنت؟**
I'm from ...	ana min ... **أنا من ...**
What do you do for a living?	māða taʻmal? **ماذا تعمل؟**
Who is this?	man haða **من هذا؟**
Who is he?	man huwa? **من هو؟**
Who is she?	man hiya? **من هي؟**
Who are they?	man hum? **من هم؟**

This is ...	haðа huwa /haðihi hiya/ ... **هذا هو /هذه هي... /**
my friend (masc.)	ṣadīqi **صديقي**
my friend (fem.)	ṣadīqati **صديقتي**
my husband	zawʒi **زوجي**
my wife	zawʒati **زوجتي**

my father	abi **أبي**
my mother	ummi **أمي**
my brother	aχi **أخي**
my son	ibni **إبني**
my daughter	ibnati **إبنتي**

This is our son.	haða huwa ibnuna **هذا هو ابننا**
This is our daughter.	haðihi hiya ibnatuna **هذه هي ابنتنا**
These are my children.	ha'ulā' awlādi **هؤلاء أولادي**
These are our children.	ha'ulā' awlāduna **هؤلاء أولادنا**

Farewells

Good bye!	as salāmu 'alaykum السلام عليكم
Bye! (inform.)	ma' as salāma مع السلامة
See you tomorrow.	ilal liqā' ɣadan إلى اللقاء غدا
See you soon.	ilal liqā' إلى اللقاء
See you at seven.	ilal liqā' as sā'a as sābi'a إلى اللقاء الساعة السابعة
Have fun!	atamanna laka waqtan ṭayyiban! أتمنى لكم وقتا طيبا!
Talk to you later.	ukallimuka lāḥiqan أكلمك لاحقا
Have a nice weekend.	'uṭlat usbū' sa'īda عطلة أسبوع سعيدة
Good night.	taṣbaḥ 'ala ɣayr تصبح على خير
It's time for me to go.	innahu waqt ðahābi إنه وقت ذهابي
I have to go.	yaʒib 'alayya an aðhab يجب علي أن أذهب
I will be right back.	sa'a'ūd ḥālan سأعود حالا
It's late.	al waqt muta'aɣɣar الوقت متأخر
I have to get up early.	yaʒib 'alayya an anhaḍ bākiran يجب علي أن أنهض باكرا
I'm leaving tomorrow.	innani uɣādir ɣadan إنني أغادر غدا
We're leaving tomorrow.	innana nuɣādir ɣadan إننا نغادر غدا
Have a nice trip!	riḥla sa'īda! رحلة سعيدة!
It was nice meeting you.	furṣa sa'īda فرصة سعيدة
It was nice talking to you.	kān laṭīf at taḥadduθ ma'ak كان لطيفا التحدث معك
Thanks for everything.	ʃukran 'ala kull ʃay' شكرا على كل شيء

I had a very good time.	qaḍayt waqt ʒayyidan **قضيت وقتا جيدا**
We had a very good time.	qaḍayna waqt ʒayyidan **قضينا وقتا جيدا**
It was really great.	kull ʃay' kān rā'i' **كل شيء كان رائعا**
I'm going to miss you.	sa'aʃtāq ilayk **سأشتاق إليك**
We're going to miss you.	sanaʃtāq ilayk **سنشتاق إليك**

Good luck!	bit tawfīq! ma' as salāma! **!مع السلامة !بالتوفيق**
Say hi to ...	taḥīyyāti li ... **تحياتي لـ...**

Foreign language

I don't understand.	ana la afham أنا لا أفهم
Write it down, please.	uktubha min faḍlak إكتبها من فضلك
Do you speak ...?	hal tatakallam bi ...? هل تتكلم بـ...؟
I speak a little bit of ...	atakallam bi ... qalīlan أتكلم بـ ... قليلا
English	al inʒlīziyya الإنجليزية
Turkish	at turkiyya التركية
Arabic	al ʿarabiyya العربية
French	al faransiyya الفرنسية
German	al almāniyya الألمانية
Italian	al itāliyya الإيطالية
Spanish	al isbāniyya الإسبانية
Portuguese	al burtuɣāliyya البرتغالية
Chinese	aṣ ṣīniyya الصينية
Japanese	al yabāniyya اليابانية
Can you repeat that, please.	hal yumkinuka tikrār min faḍlak? هل يمكنك تكرار من فضلك؟
I understand.	ana afham انا أفهم
I don't understand.	ana la afham أنا لا أفهم
Please speak more slowly.	takallam bi buṭʾ akθar min faḍlak تكلم ببطء أكثر من فضلك
Is that correct? (Am I saying it right?)	hal haða ṣaḥīḥ? هل هذا صحيح؟
What is this? (What does this mean?)	māða yaʿni? ماذا يعني؟

Apologies

Excuse me, please.	la tu'āχiðni min faḍlak **لا تؤاخذني من فضلك**
I'm sorry.	ana 'āṣif **أنا آسف**
I'm really sorry.	ana 'āsif ʒiddan **أنا آسف جدا**
Sorry, it's my fault.	ana 'āsif innaha ɣalṭati **أنا آسف، إنها غلطتي**
My mistake.	χaṭa'i **خطئي**

May I ...?	hal yumkinuni ...? **هل يمكنني ...؟**
Do you mind if I ...?	hal tumāni' law ...? **هل تمانع لو ...؟**
It's OK.	laysa hunāk ayy muʃkila **ليس هناك أي مشكلة**
It's all right.	kull ʃay' 'ala ma yurām **كل شيء على ما يرام**
Don't worry about it.	la taqlaq **لا تقلق**

Agreement

Yes.	na'am نعم
Yes, sure.	aʒl أجل
OK (Good!)	ḥasanan حسنا
Very well.	ʒayyid ʒiddan جيد جدا
Certainly!	bit ta'kīd! !بالتأكيد
I agree.	ana muwāfiq أنا موافق
That's correct.	haða ṣaḥīḥ هذا صحيح
That's right.	haða ṣaḥīḥ هذا صحيح
You're right.	kalāmak ṣaḥīḥ كلامك صحيح
I don't mind.	ana la umāni' أنا لا أمانع
Absolutely right.	anta muḥiqq tamāman أنت محق تماما
It's possible.	innahu min al mumkin إنه من الممكن
That's a good idea.	innaha fikra ʒayyida إنها فكرة جيدة
I can't say no.	la astaṭī' an aqūl la لا أستطيع أن أقول لا
I'd be happy to.	sa'akūn sa'īdan سأكون سعيدا
With pleasure.	bi kull surūr بكل سرور

Refusal. Expressing doubt

No.	la **لا**
Certainly not.	tabʿan la **طبعا لا**
I don't agree.	lastu muwāfiq **لست موافقا**
I don't think so.	la aẓunn ðalika **لا أظن ذلك**
It's not true.	laysa haða ṣaḥīḥ **ليس هذا صحيحا**
You are wrong.	aχṭaʾta **أخطأت**
I think you are wrong.	aẓunn annaka aχṭaʾt **أظن أنك أخطأت**
I'm not sure.	lastu mutaʾakkid **لست متأكدا**
It's impossible.	haða mustaḥīl **هذا مستحيل**
Nothing of the kind (sort)!	la ʃayʾ min haðan nawʿ **لا شيء من هذا النوع**
The exact opposite.	al ʿaks tamāman **العكس تماما**
I'm against it.	ana ḍidda ðalika **أنا ضد ذلك**
I don't care.	la yuhimmuni ðalika **لا يهمني ذلك**
I have no idea.	laysa ladayya ayy fikra **ليس لدي أي فكرة**
I doubt it.	aʃukk fe ðalik **أشك في ذلك**
Sorry, I can't.	ʾāsif la astaṭīʿ **آسف، لا أستطيع**
Sorry, I don't want to.	ʾāsif la urīd ðalika **آسف، لا أريد ذلك**
Thank you, but I don't need this.	ʃukran, wa lakinnani la aḥtāʒ ila ðalika **شكرا، ولكنني لا أحتاج إلى ذلك**
It's getting late.	al waqt mutaʾaχχar **الوقت متأخر**

I have to get up early.	yaʒib ʿalayya an anhaḍ bākiran **يجب علي أن أنهض باكرا**
I don't feel well.	la aʃʿur bi χayr **لا أشعر بخير**

Expressing gratitude

Thank you.	ʃukran شكرا
Thank you very much.	ʃukran ʒazīlan شكرا جزيلا
I really appreciate it.	ana uqaddir ðalika ḥaqqan أنا أقدر ذلك حقا
I'm really grateful to you.	ana mumtann lak ʒiddan أنا ممتن لك جدا
We are really grateful to you.	naḥnu mumtannīn lak ʒiddan نحن ممتنون لك جدا

Thank you for your time.	ʃukran ʿala waqtak شكرا على وقتك
Thanks for everything.	ʃukran ʿala kull ʃayʾ شكرا على كل شيء
Thank you for ...	ʃukran ʿala ... شكرا على ...
your help	musāʿadatak مساعدتك
a nice time	al waqt al laṭīf الوقت اللطيف

---

a wonderful meal	waʒba rāʾiʿa وجبة رائعة
a pleasant evening	amsiyya mumtiʿa أمسية ممتعة
a wonderful day	yawm rāʾiʿ يوم رائع
an amazing journey	riḥla mudhiʃa رحلة مدهشة

Don't mention it.	la ʃukr ʿala wāʒib لا شكر على واجب
You are welcome.	al ʿafw العفو
Any time.	fi ayy waqt في أي وقت
My pleasure.	bi kull surūr بكل سرور
Forget it.	insa al amr إنس الأمر
Don't worry about it.	la taqlaq لا تقلق

Congratulations. Best wishes

Congratulations!	uhanni'uka! أهنئك!
Happy birthday!	ʿīd milād saʿīd! عيد ميلاد سعيد!
Merry Christmas!	ʿīd milād saʿīd! عيد ميلاد سعيد!
Happy New Year!	sana ʒadīda saʿīda! سنة جديدة سعيدة!
Happy Easter!	ʿīd fiṣḥ saʿīd! عيد فصح سعيد!
Happy Hanukkah!	hanūka saʿīda! هانوكا سعيدة!
I'd like to propose a toast.	awudd an aqtariḥ naχb أود أن أقترح نخبا
Cheers!	fi siḥḥatak في صحتك
Let's drink to ...!	da'awna naʃrab fi ...! دعونا نشرب في ...!
To our success!	naʒāḥna نجاحنا
To your success!	naʒāḥak نجاحك
Good luck!	bit tawfīq! بالتوفيق!
Have a nice day!	atamanna laka nahāran saʿīdan! أتمنى لك نهارا سعيدا!
Have a good holiday!	atamanna laka ʿuṭla ṭayyiba! أتمنى لك عطلة طيبة!
Have a safe journey!	atamanna laka riḥla āmina! أتمنى لك رحلة آمنة!
I hope you get better soon!	atamanna bi annaka satataḥassan qarīban أتمنى بأنك ستتحسن قريبا

Socializing

Why are you sad?	limāða anta ḥazīn? لماذا أنت حزين؟
Smile! Cheer up!	ibtasim! إبتسم!
Are you free tonight?	hal anta ḥurr haðihil layla? هل أنت حر هذه الليلة؟
May I offer you a drink?	hal tawudd an taʃrab ʃay'? هل تود أن تشرب شيئا؟
Would you like to dance?	hal tawudd an tarquṣ? هل تود أن ترقص؟
Let's go to the movies.	da'awna naðhab ilas sinima دعونا نذهب إلى السينما
May I invite you to ...?	hal yumkinuni an ad'ūk ila ...? هل يمكنني أن أدعوك إلى ...؟
a restaurant	maṭ'am مطعم
the movies	as sinima السينما
the theater	al masraḥ المسرح
go for a walk	tamʃiya تمشية
At what time?	fi ayy sā'a? في أي ساعة؟
tonight	haðal masā' هذا المساء
at six	as sā'a as sādisa الساعة السادسة
at seven	as sā'a as sābi'a الساعة السابعة
at eight	as sā'a aθ θāmina الساعة الثامنة
at nine	as sā'a at tāsi'a الساعة التاسعة
Do you like it here?	hal yu'ʒibak al makān? هل يعجبك المكان؟
Are you here with someone?	hal anta huna ma' aḥad? هل أنت هنا مع أحد؟
I'm with my friend.	ana ma' ṣadīq أنا مع صديق

I'm with my friends.	ana ma' aṣdiqā' أنا مع أصدقاء
No, I'm alone.	la, ana li waḥdi لا، أنا لوحدي

Do you have a boyfriend?	hal 'indak ṣadīq? هل عندك صديق؟
I have a boyfriend.	ana 'indi ṣadīq أنا عندي صديق
Do you have a girlfriend?	hal 'indak ṣadīqa? هل عندك صديقة؟
I have a girlfriend.	ana 'indi ṣadīqa أنا عندي صديقة

Can I see you again?	hal yumkinuni ru'yatak marra uxra? هل يمكنني رؤيتك مرة أخرى؟
Can I call you?	hal astaṭī' an attaṣil bik? هل أستطيع أن أتصل بك؟
Call me. (Give me a call.)	ittaṣil bi إتصل بي
What's your number?	ma raqmak? ما رقمك؟
I miss you.	aʃtāq ilayk أشتاق إليك

You have a beautiful name.	ismak ʒamīl إسمك جميل
I love you.	uḥibbak أحبك
Will you marry me?	hal tatazawwaʒīnani? هل تتزوجينني؟
You're kidding!	anta tamzaḥ! أنت تمزح!
I'm just kidding.	ana amzaḥ faqaṭ أنا أمزح فقط

Are you serious?	hal anta gadd? هل أنت جاد؟
I'm serious.	ana gādd أنا جاد
Really?!	ṣaḥīḥ? صحيح؟
It's unbelievable!	haða ɣayr ma'qūl! هذا غير معقول!
I don't believe you.	la uṣaddiqak لا أصدقك
I can't.	ana la astaṭī' أنا لا أستطيع
I don't know.	la a'rif أنا لا أعرف
I don't understand you.	la afhamak أنا لا أفهمك

Please go away.	min faḍlak iðhab min huna **من فضلك إذهب من هنا**
Leave me alone!	utrukni li waḥdi! **أتركني لوحدي!**

I can't stand him.	ana la uṭīquhu **أنا لا أطيقه**
You are disgusting!	anta muqrif **أنت مقرف**
I'll call the police!	ḥaṭṭlob el ʃorṭa **سأتصل بالشرطة**

Sharing impressions. Emotions

I like it.	yu'ʒibuni ðalika **يعجبني ذلك**
Very nice.	ʒamīl ʒiddan **جميل جداً**
That's great!	haða rā'i' **هذا رائع**
It's not bad.	la ba's bihi **لا بأس به**
I don't like it.	la yu'ʒibuni ðalika **لا يعجبني ذلك**
It's not good.	laysa ʒayyid **ليس جيداً**
It's bad.	haða sayyi' **هذا سيء**
It's very bad.	haða sayyi' ʒiddan **هذا سيء جداً**
It's disgusting.	haða muqrif **هذا مقرف**
I'm happy.	ana sa'īd /sa'īda/ **أنا سعيد /سعيدة/**
I'm content.	ana mabsūṭ /mabsūṭa/ **أنا مبسوط /مبسوطة/**
I'm in love.	ana uḥibb **أنا أحب**
I'm calm.	ana hādi' /hādi'a/ **أنا هادئ /هادئة/**
I'm bored.	aʃur bil malal **أشعر بالملل**
I'm tired.	ana ta'bān /ta'bāna/ **أنا تعبان /تعبانة/**
I'm sad.	ana ḥazīn /ḥazīna/ **أنا حزين /حزينة/**
I'm frightened.	ana χā'if /χā'ifa/ **أنا خائف /خائفة/**
I'm angry.	ana ɣāḍib /ɣāḍiba/ **أنا غاضب /غاضبة/**
I'm worried.	ana qaliq /qaliqa/ **أنا قلق /قلقة/**
I'm nervous.	ana mutawattir /mutawattira/ **أنا متوتر /متوترة/**

I'm jealous. (envious)	ana ɣayūr /ɣayūra/ **أنا غيور /غيورة/**
I'm surprised.	ana mutafāʒi' /mutafāʒi'a/ **أنا متفاجئ /متفاجئة/**
I'm perplexed.	ana ḥā'ir /ḥā'ira/ **أنا حائر /حائرة/**

Problems. Accidents

I've got a problem.	ʿindi muʃkila	عندي مشكلة
We've got a problem.	ʿindana muʃkila	عندنا مشكلة
I'm lost.	aḍaʿt ṭarīqi	أضعت طريقي
I missed the last bus (train).	fātatni 'āχir ḥāfila	فاتتني آخر حافلة
I don't have any money left.	laysa ladayya ayy māl	ليس لدي أي مال
I've lost my ...	faqadt ...	فقدت ...
Someone stole my ...	saraqu minni ...	سرقوا مني ...
passport	ʒawāz as safar	جواز السفر
wallet	al mahfaẓa	المحفظة
papers	al awrāq	الأوراق
ticket	at taðkira	التذكرة
money	an nuqūd	النقود
handbag	aʃ ʃanṭa	الشنطة
camera	al kamira	الكاميرا
laptop	al kumbyūtir al maḥmūl	الكمبيوتر المحمول
tablet computer	al kumbyūtir al lawḥiy	الكمبيوتر اللوحى
mobile phone	at tilifūn al maḥmūl	التليفون المحمول
Help me!	sāʿidni!	ساعدني!
What's happened?	māða ḥadaθ?	ماذا حدث؟
fire	ḥarīqa	حريقة

shooting	iṭlāq an nār **إطلاق النار**
murder	qatl **قتل**
explosion	infiʒār **إنفجار**
fight	χināqa **خناقة**

Call the police!	ittaṣil biʃ ʃurṭa! **إتّصل بالشرطة!**
Please hurry up!	bi surʿa min faḍlak! **بسرعة من فضلك!**
I'm looking for the police station.	abḥaθ ʿan qism aʃ ʃurṭa **أبحث عن قسم الشرطة**
I need to make a call.	urīd iʒrāʾ mukālama hātifiyya **أريد إجراء مكالمة هاتفية**
May I use your phone?	hal yumkinuni an astaχdim tilifūnak? **هل يمكنني أن أستخدم تليفونك؟**

I've been …	laqat taʿarraḍt li … **لقد تعرضت لـ...**
mugged	sirqa **سرقة**
robbed	sirqa **سرقة**
raped	iɣtiṣāb **إغتصاب**
attacked (beaten up)	iʿtidāʾ **إعتداء**

Are you all right?	hal anta bi χayr? **هل أنت بخير؟**
Did you see who it was?	hal raʾayt man kān ðalik? **هل رأيت من كان ذلك؟**
Would you be able to recognize the person?	hal tastaṭīʿ at taʿarruf ʿalayhi? **هل ستستطيع التعرف عليه؟**
Are you sure?	hal anta mutaʾkked? **هل أنت متأكد؟**

Please calm down.	ihdaʾ min faḍlak **إهدأ من فضلك**
Take it easy!	hawwin ʿalayk! **هون عليك!**
Don't worry!	la taqlaq! **لا تقلق!**
Everything will be fine.	kull ʃayʾ sayakūn ʿala ma yurām **كل شيء سيكون على ما يرام**
Everything's all right.	kull ʃayʾ ʿala ma yurām **كل شيء على ما يرام**
Come here, please.	taʿāla huna law samaḥt **تعال هنا لو سمحت**

I have some questions for you.	ʻindi lak as'ila عندي لك أسئلة
Wait a moment, please.	intaẓir laḥẓa min faḍlak إنتظر لحظة من فضلك
Do you have any I.D.?	hal ʻindak biṭāqa ʃaχsiyya? هل عندك بطاقة شخصية؟
Thanks. You can leave now.	ʃukran. yumkinuka al muɣādara al 'ān شكرا. يمكنك المغادرة الآن
Hands behind your head!	ḍaʻ yadayk χalfa ra'sak! ضع يديك خلف رأسك!
You're under arrest!	anta mawqūf! أنت موقوف!

Health problems

Please help me.	sāʿidni min faḍlak ساعدني من فضلق
I don't feel well.	la aʃur bi χayr لا أشعر بخير
My husband doesn't feel well.	zawʒi la yaʃur bi χayr زوجي لا يشعر بخير
My son ...	ibni ... إبني ...
My father ...	abi ... أبي ...
My wife doesn't feel well.	zawʒati la taʃur bi χayr زوجتي لا تشعر بخير
My daughter ...	ibnati ... إبنتي ...
My mother ...	ummi ... أمي ...
I've got a ...	ana ʿindi ... أنا عندي ...
headache	ṣudāʿ صداع
sore throat	iltihāb fil ḥalq إلتهاب في الحلق
stomach ache	maɣaṣ مغص
toothache	alam asnān ألم أسنان
I feel dizzy.	aʃur bid dawār أشعر بالدوار
He has a fever.	ʿindahu ḥumma عنده حمى
She has a fever.	ʿindaha ḥumma عندها حمى
I can't breathe.	la astaṭīʿ at tanaffus لا أستطيع التنفس
I'm short of breath.	aʃur bi ḍīq at tanaffus أشعر بضيق التنفس
I am asthmatic.	uʿāni min ar rabw أعاني من الربو
I am diabetic.	ana ʿindi maraḍ as sukkar أنا عندي مرض السكر

I can't sleep.	la astaṭīʿ an anām **لا أستطيع أن أنام**
food poisoning	tasammum ɣiðā'iy **تسمم غذائي**

It hurts here.	aʃur bi alam huna **أشعر بألم هنا**
Help me!	sāʿidni! **ساعدني!**
I am here!	ana huna! **أنا هنا!**
We are here!	naḥnu huna! **نحن هنا!**
Get me out of here!	aχraʒūni min huna **أخرجوني من هنا!**
I need a doctor.	ana aḥtāʒ ila ṭabīb **أنا أحتاج إلى طبيب**
I can't move.	la astaṭīʿ an ataharrak **لا أستطيع أن أتحرك**
I can't move my legs.	la astaṭīʿ an uharrik riʒlayya **لا أستطيع أن أحرك رجلي**

I have a wound.	ʿindi ʒurḥ **عندي جرح**
Is it serious?	hal al amr χaṭīr? **هل الأمر خطير؟**
My documents are in my pocket.	awrāqi fi ʒaybi **أوراقي في جيبي**
Calm down!	ihda'! **إهدأ!**
May I use your phone?	hal yumkinuni an astaχdim tilifūnak? **هل يمكنني أن أستخدم تليفونك؟**

Call an ambulance!	ittaṣil bil isʿāf! **إتصل بالإسعاف!**
It's urgent!	al amr ʿāʒil! **الأمر عاجل!**
It's an emergency!	innaha ḥāla ṭāri'a! **إنها حالة طارئة!**
Please hurry up!	bi surʿa min faḍlak! **بسرعة من فضلك!**
Would you please call a doctor?	ittaṣil biṭ ṭabib min faḍlak? **إتصل بالطبيب من فضلك**
Where is the hospital?	ayna al mustaʃfa? **أين المستشفى؟**

How are you feeling?	kayf taʃur al 'ān **كيف تشعر الآن؟**
Are you all right?	hal anta bi χayr? **هل أنت بخير؟**
What's happened?	māða hadaθ? **ماذا حدث؟**

I feel better now.	aʃur bi taḥassun al 'ān **أشعر بتحسن الآن**
It's OK.	la ba's **لا بأس**
It's all right.	kull ʃay' 'ala ma yurām **كل شيء على ما يرام**

At the pharmacy

pharmacy (drugstore)	ṣaydaliyya **صيدلية**
24-hour pharmacy	ṣaydaliyya arba' wa 'iʃrīn sā'a **صيدلية 24 ساعة**
Where is the closest pharmacy?	ayna aqrab ṣaydaliyya? **أين أقرب صيدلية؟**
Is it open now?	hal hiya maftūḥa al 'ān? **هل هي مفتوحة الآن؟**
At what time does it open?	mata taftaḥ? **متى تفتح؟**
At what time does it close?	mata tuɣliq? **متى تغلق؟**
Is it far?	hal hiya ba'īda? **هل هي بعيدة؟**
Can I get there on foot?	hal yumkinuni an aṣil ila hunāk māʃiyan? **هل يمكنني أن أصل إلى هناك ماشيا؟**
Can you show me on the map?	arīni 'alal ɣarīṭa min faḍlak **أريني على الخريطة من فضلك**
Please give me something for …	min faḍlak a'ṭini ʃay' li … **من فضلك أعطني شيئا لـ...**
a headache	aṣ ṣudā' **الصداع**
a cough	as su'āl **السعال**
a cold	al bard **البرد**
the flu	al influenza **الأنفلوانزا**
a fever	al ḥumma **الحمى**
a stomach ache	el maɣaṣ **المغص**
nausea	a ɣaθayān **الغثيان**
diarrhea	al ishāl **الإسهال**
constipation	al imsāk **الإمساك**
pain in the back	alam fiz ẓahr **ألم في الظهر**

chest pain	alam fiṣ ṣadr **ألم في الصدر**
side stitch	ɣurza ʒānibiyya **غرزة جانبية**
abdominal pain	alam fil baṭn **ألم في البطن**

pill	ḥabba **حبة**
ointment, cream	marham, krīm **مرهم، كريم**
syrup	ʃarāb **شراب**
spray	baχχāχ **بخاخ**
drops	qaṭarāt **قطرات**

You need to go to the hospital.	ʿalayk an taðhab ilal mustaʃfa **عليك أن تذهب إلى المستشفى**
health insurance	ta'mīn ṣiḥḥiy **تأمين صحي**
prescription	waṣfa ṭibbiyya **وصفة طبية**
insect repellant	ṭārid lil ḥaʃarāt **طارد للحشرات**
Band Aid	laṣqa lil ʒurūḥ **لصقة للجروح**

The bare minimum

Excuse me, ...	law samaḥt, ... **لو سمحت، ...**
Hello.	as salāmu 'alaykum **السلام عليكم**
Thank you.	ʃukran **شكرا**
Good bye.	ma' as salāma **مع السلامة**
Yes.	na'am **نعم**
No.	la **لا**
I don't know.	la a'rif **لا أعرف**
Where? | Where to? | When?	ayna? | ila ayna? | mata? **أين؟ | إلى أين؟ | متى؟**
I need ...	ana aḥtāʒ ila ... **أنا أحتاج إلى...**
I want ...	ana urīd ... **أنا أريد ...**
Do you have ...?	hal 'indak ...? **هل عندك... ؟**
Is there a ... here?	hal yūʒad huna ...? **هل يوجد هنا ...؟**
May I ...?	hal yumkinuni ...? **هل يمكنني...؟**
..., please (polite request)	... min faḍlak **من فضلك ...**
I'm looking for ...	abḥaθ 'an ... **أبحث عن ...**
restroom	ḥammām **حمام**
ATM	mākīnat ṣarrāf 'āliy **ماكينة صراف آلي**
pharmacy (drugstore)	ṣaydaliyya **صيدلية**
hospital	mustaʃfa **مستشفى**
police station	qism aʃ ʃurṭa **قسم شرطة**
subway	mitru al anfāq **مترو الأنفاق**

taxi	taksi **تاكسي**
train station	mahattat al qiṭār **محطة القطار**

My name is ...	ismi ... **إسمي...**
What's your name?	ma smuka? **ما اسمك؟**
Could you please help me?	sāʿidni min faḍlak **ساعدني من فضلك**
I've got a problem.	ʿindi muʃkila **عندي مشكلة**
I don't feel well.	la aʃʿur bi χayr **لا أشعر بخير**
Call an ambulance!	ittaṣil bil isʿāf! **إتصل بالإسعاف!**
May I make a call?	hal yumkinuni iʒrāʾ mukālama tilifūniyya? **هل يمكنني إجراء مكالمة هاتفية؟**

I'm sorry.	ana ʾāṣif **أنا آسف**
You're welcome.	al ʿafw **العفو**

I, me	ana **أنا**
you (inform.)	anta **أنت**
he	huwa **هو**
she	hiya **هي**
they (masc.)	hum **هم**
they (fem.)	hum **هم**
we	naḥnu **نحن**
you (pl)	antum **أنتم**
you (sg, form.)	ḥaḍritak **حضرتك**

ENTRANCE	duχūl **دخول**
EXIT	χurūʒ **خروج**
OUT OF ORDER	muʿaṭṭal **معطل**
CLOSED	muɣlaq **مغلق**

OPEN	maftūḥ **مفتوح**
FOR WOMEN	lis sayyidāt **للسيدات**
FOR MEN	lir riʒāl **للرجال**

TOPICAL VOCABULARY

This section contains more than 3,000 of the most important words.
The dictionary will provide invaluable assistance while traveling abroad, because frequently individual words are enough for you to be understood.
The dictionary includes a convenient transcription of each foreign word

T&P Books Publishing

VOCABULARY CONTENTS

T&P Books Publishing

BASIC CONCEPTS

T&P Books Publishing

1. Pronouns

I, me	ana	أنا
you (masc.)	enta	أنت
you (fem.)	enty	أنت
he	howwa	هوّ
she	hiya	هيّ
we	eḥna	إحنا
you (to a group)	antom	أنتم
they	hamm	همّ

2. Greetings. Salutations

Hello! (form.)	assalamu ʿalaykum!	السلام عليكم!
Good morning!	ṣabāḥ el χeyr!	صباح الخير!
Good afternoon!	neharak saʿīd!	نهارك سعيد!
Good evening!	masāʾ el χeyr!	مساء الخير!
to say hello	sallem	سلّم
Hi! (hello)	ahlan!	أهلاً!
greeting (n)	salām (m)	سلام
to greet (vt)	sallem ʿala	سلّم على
How are you?	ezzayek?	ازّيك؟
What's new?	aχbārak eyh?	أخبارك ايه؟
Bye-Bye! Goodbye!	maʿ el salāma!	مع السلامة!
See you soon!	aʃūfak orayeb!	أشوفك قريب!
Farewell!	maʿ el salāma!	مع السلامة!
to say goodbye	waddaʿ	ودّع
So long!	bay bay!	باي باي!
Thank you!	ʃokran!	شكراً!
Thank you very much!	ʃokran geddan!	شكراً جداً!
You're welcome	el ʿafw	العفو
Don't mention it!	la ʃokr ʿala wāgeb	لا شكر على واجب
It was nothing	el ʿafw	العفو
Excuse me! (fam.)	ʿan eznak!	عن إذنك!
Excuse me! (form.)	baʿd ezn ḥadretak!	بعد إذن حضرتك!
to excuse (forgive)	ʿazar	عذر
to apologize (vi)	eʿtazar	أعتذر
My apologies	ana ʾāsef	أنا آسف

I'm sorry!	ana ʾāsef!	!أنا آسف
to forgive (vt)	ʿafa	عفا
please (adv)	men faḍlak	من فضلك
Don't forget!	ma tensāʃ!	!ما تنساش
Certainly!	ṭabʿan!	!طبعاً
Of course not!	laʾ ṭabʿan!	!لأ طبعاً
Okay! (I agree)	ettafaʾna!	!إتّفقنا
That's enough!	kefāya!	!كفاية

3. Questions

Who?	mīn?	مين؟
What?	eyh?	ايه؟
Where? (at, in)	feyn?	فين؟
Where (to)?	feyn?	فين؟
From where?	meneyn?	منين؟
When?	emta	امتى؟
Why? (What for?)	ʿaʃān eyh?	عشان ايه؟
Why? (~ are you crying?)	leyh?	ليه؟
What for?	l eyh?	لـ ليه؟
How? (in what way)	ezāy?	إزاي؟
What? (What kind of …?)	eyh?	ايه؟
Which?	ayī?	أيّ؟
To whom?	le mīn?	لمين؟
About whom?	ʿan mīn?	عن مين؟
About what?	ʿan eyh?	عن ايه؟
With whom?	maʿ mīn?	مع مين؟
How many? How much?	kām?	كام؟
Whose?	betāʿet mīn?	بتاعت مين؟

4. Prepositions

with (accompanied by)	maʿ	مع
without	men ɣeyr	من غير
to (indicating direction)	ela	إلى
about (talking ~ …)	ʿan	عن
before (in time)	ʾabl	قبل
in front of …	ʾoddām	قدّام
under (beneath, below)	taḥt	تحت
above (over)	foʾe	فوق
on (atop)	ʿala	على
from (off, out of)	men	من
of (made from)	men	من

in (e.g., ~ ten minutes)	baʿd	بعد
over (across the top of)	men ʿala	من على

5. Function words. Adverbs. Part 1

Where? (at, in)	feyn?	فين؟
here (adv)	hena	هنا
there (adv)	henāk	هناك
somewhere (to be)	fe makānen ma	في مكان ما
nowhere (not anywhere)	meʃ fi ayī makān	مش في أيّ مكان
by (near, beside)	ganb	جنب
by the window	ganb el ʃebbāk	جنب الشبّاك
Where (to)?	feyn?	فين؟
here (e.g., come ~!)	hena	هنا
there (e.g., to go ~)	henāk	هناك
from here (adv)	men hena	من هنا
from there (adv)	men henāk	من هناك
close (adv)	ʾarīb	قريب
far (adv)	beʿīd	بعيد
near (e.g., ~ Paris)	ʿand	عند
nearby (adv)	ʾarīb	قريب
not far (adv)	meʃ beʿīd	مش بعيد
left (adj)	el ʃemāl	الشمال
on the left	ʿalal ʃemāl	على الشمال
to the left	lel ʃemāl	للشمال
right (adj)	el yemīn	اليمين
on the right	ʿalal yemīn	على اليمين
to the right	lel yemīn	لليمين
in front (adv)	ʾoddām	قدّام
front (as adj)	amāmy	أمامي
ahead (the kids ran ~)	ela el amām	إلى الأمام
behind (adv)	waraʾ	وراء
from behind	men wara	من وَرا
back (towards the rear)	le wara	لوَرا
middle	wasaṭ (m)	وسط
in the middle	fel wasat	في الوسط
at the side	ʿala ganb	على جنب
everywhere (adv)	fe kol makān	في كل مكان
around (in all directions)	ḥawaleyn	حوالين
from inside	men gowwah	من جوه

somewhere (to go)	le ʾayī makān	لأي مكان
straight (directly)	ʿala ṭūl	على طول
back (e.g., come ~)	rogūʿ	رجوع
from anywhere	men ayī makān	من أيّ مكان
from somewhere	men makānen mā	من مكان ما
firstly (adv)	awwalan	أوّلاً
secondly (adv)	sāneyan	ثانياً
thirdly (adv)	sālesan	ثالثاً
suddenly (adv)	fagʾa	فجأة
at first (in the beginning)	fel bedāya	في البداية
for the first time	le ʾawwel marra	لأوّل مرّة
long before ...	ʾabl ... be modda ṭawīla	بمدة طويلة ...قبل
anew (over again)	men gedīd	من جديد
for good (adv)	lel abad	للأبد
never (adv)	abadan	أبداً
again (adv)	tāny	تاني
now (adv)	delwaʾty	دلوقتي
often (adv)	ketīr	كثير
then (adv)	waʾtaha	وقتها
urgently (quickly)	ʿala ṭūl	على طول
usually (adv)	ʿādatan	عادةً
by the way, ...	ʿala fekra ...	...على فكرة
possible (that is ~)	momken	ممكن
probably (adv)	momken	ممكن
maybe (adv)	momken	ممكن
besides ...	bel eḍāfa ela ...	...بالإضافة إلى
that's why ...	ʿaʃān keda	عشان كده
in spite of ...	bel raɣm men ...	...بالرغم من
thanks to ...	be faḍl ...	...بفضل
what (pron.)	elly	إللي
that (conj.)	ennu	إنّه
something	ḥāga (f)	حاجة
anything (something)	ayī ḥāga (f)	أيّ حاجة
nothing	wala ḥāga	ولا حاجة
who (pron.)	elly	إللي
someone	ḥadd	حدّ
somebody	ḥadd	حدّ
nobody	wala ḥadd	ولا حدّ
nowhere (a voyage to ~)	meʃ le wala makān	مش لـ ولا مكان
nobody's	wala ḥadd	ولا حدّ
somebody's	le ḥadd	لحدّ
so (I'm ~ glad)	geddan	جداً
also (as well)	kamān	كمان
too (as well)	kamān	كمان

6. Function words. Adverbs. Part 2

Why?	leyh?	ليه؟
for some reason	le sabeben ma	لسبب ما
because ...	ʿaʃān ...	عشان ...
for some purpose	le hadafen mā	لهدف ما
and	w	و
or	walla	ولّا
but	bass	بسّ
for (e.g., ~ me)	ʿaʃān	عشان
too (~ many people)	ketīr geddan	كتير جدّاً
only (exclusively)	bass	بسّ
exactly (adv)	bel ḍabṭ	بالضبط
about (more or less)	naḥw	نحو
approximately (adv)	naḥw	نحو
approximate (adj)	taqrīby	تقريبي
almost (adv)	ta'rīban	تقريباً
the rest	el bā'y (m)	الباقي
each (adj)	koll	كلّ
any (no matter which)	ayī	أيّ
many, much (a lot of)	ketīr	كتير
many people	nās ketīr	ناس كتير
all (everyone)	koll el nās	كلّ الناس
in return for ...	fi moqābel ...	في مقابل ...
in exchange (adv)	fe moqābel	في مقابل
by hand (made)	bel yad	باليد
hardly (negative opinion)	bel kād	بالكاد
probably (adv)	momken	ممكن
on purpose (intentionally)	bel 'aṣd	بالقصد
by accident (adv)	bel ṣodfa	بالصدفة
very (adv)	'awy	قوّي
for example (adv)	masalan	مثلاً
between	beyn	بين
among	wesṭ	وسط
so much (such a lot)	ketīr	كتير
especially (adv)	χāṣṣa	خاصّة

NUMBERS. MISCELLANEOUS

T&P Books Publishing

7. Cardinal numbers. Part 1

0 zero	ṣefr	صفر
1 one	wāḥed	واحد
1 one (fem.)	waḥda	واحدة
2 two	etneyn	إتنين
3 three	talāta	ثلاثة
4 four	arbaʿa	أربعة
5 five	χamsa	خمسة
6 six	setta	ستّة
7 seven	sabʿa	سبعة
8 eight	tamanya	ثمانية
9 nine	tesʿa	تسعة
10 ten	ʿaʃara	عشرة
11 eleven	ḥedāʃar	حداشر
12 twelve	etnāʃar	إتناشر
13 thirteen	talattāʃar	تلاتّاشر
14 fourteen	arbaʿtāʃer	أربعتاشر
15 fifteen	χamastāʃer	خمستاشر
16 sixteen	settāʃar	ستّاشر
17 seventeen	sabaʿtāʃar	سبعتاشر
18 eighteen	tamantāʃar	تمنتاشر
19 nineteen	tesʿatāʃar	تسعتاشر
20 twenty	ʿeʃrīn	عشرين
21 twenty-one	wāḥed we ʿeʃrīn	واحد وعشرين
22 twenty-two	etneyn we ʿeʃrīn	إتنين وعشرين
23 twenty-three	talāta we ʿeʃrīn	ثلاثة وعشرين
30 thirty	talatīn	ثلاثين
31 thirty-one	wāḥed we talatīn	واحد وتلاتين
32 thirty-two	etneyn we talatīn	إتنين وتلاتين
33 thirty-three	talāta we talatīn	ثلاثة وثلاثين
40 forty	arbeʿīn	أربعين
41 forty-one	wāḥed we arbeʿīn	واحد وأربعين
42 forty-two	etneyn we arbeʿīn	إتنين وأربعين
43 forty-three	talāta we arbeʿīn	ثلاثة وأربعين
50 fifty	χamsīn	خمسين
51 fifty-one	wāḥed we χamsīn	واحد وخمسين
52 fifty-two	etneyn we χamsīn	إتنين وخمسين
53 fifty-three	talāta we χamsīn	ثلاثة وخمسين

60 sixty	settīn	ستّين
61 sixty-one	wāḥed we settīn	واحد وستّين
62 sixty-two	etneyn we settīn	إتنين وستّين
63 sixty-three	talāta we settīn	ثلاثة وستّين
70 seventy	sab'īn	سبعين
71 seventy-one	wāḥed we sab'īn	واحد وسبعين
72 seventy-two	etneyn we sab'īn	إتنين وسبعين
73 seventy-three	talāta we sab'īn	ثلاثة وسبعين
80 eighty	tamanīn	ثمانين
81 eighty-one	wāḥed we tamanīn	واحد وتمانين
82 eighty-two	etneyn we tamanīn	إتنين وتمانين
83 eighty-three	talāta we tamanīn	ثلاثة وثمانين
90 ninety	tes'īn	تسعين
91 ninety-one	wāḥed we tes'īn	واحد وتسعين
92 ninety-two	etneyn we tes'īn	إتنين وتسعين
93 ninety-three	talāta we tes'īn	ثلاثة وتسعين

8. Cardinal numbers. Part 2

100 one hundred	miya	ميّة
200 two hundred	meteyn	ميتين
300 three hundred	toltomiya	تلتميّة
400 four hundred	rob'omiya	ربعميّة
500 five hundred	χomsomiya	خمسميّة
600 six hundred	sotomiya	ستميّة
700 seven hundred	sob'omiya	سبعميّة
800 eight hundred	tomnome'a	ثمنمئة
900 nine hundred	tos'omiya	تسعميّة
1000 one thousand	alf	ألف
2000 two thousand	alfeyn	ألفين
3000 three thousand	talat 'ālāf	ثلاث آلاف
10000 ten thousand	'aʃaret 'ālāf	عشرة آلاف
one hundred thousand	mīt alf	ميت ألف
million	millyon (m)	مليون
billion	millyār (m)	مليار

9. Ordinal numbers

first (adj)	awwel	أوّل
second (adj)	tāny	ثاني
third (adj)	tālet	ثالث
fourth (adj)	rābe'	رابع
fifth (adj)	χāmes	خامس

sixth (adj)	sādes	سادس
seventh (adj)	sābeʿ	سابع
eighth (adj)	tāmen	ثامن
ninth (adj)	tāseʿ	تاسع
tenth (adj)	ʿāʃer	عاشر

COLOURS. UNITS OF MEASUREMENT

T&P Books Publishing

10. Colors

color	lone (m)	لون
shade (tint)	daraget el lōn (m)	درجة اللون
hue	ṣabɣet lōn (f)	صبغة اللون
rainbow	qose qozaḥ (m)	قوس قزح
white (adj)	abyaḍ	أبيض
black (adj)	aswad	أسود
gray (adj)	romādy	رمادي
green (adj)	aχḍar	أخضر
yellow (adj)	aṣfar	أصفر
red (adj)	aḥmar	أحمر
blue (adj)	azra'	أزرق
light blue (adj)	azra' fāteḥ	أزرق فاتح
pink (adj)	wardy	وردي
orange (adj)	bortoqāly	برتقاليّ
violet (adj)	banaffsegy	بنفّسجي
brown (adj)	bonny	بنّي
golden (adj)	dahaby	ذهبي
silvery (adj)	feḍḍy	فضي
beige (adj)	bɛ:ʒ	بيج
cream (adj)	'āgy	عاجيّ
turquoise (adj)	fayrūzy	فيروزي
cherry red (adj)	aḥmar karazy	أحمر كرزي
lilac (adj)	laylaky	ليّلكي
crimson (adj)	qormozy	قرمزي
light (adj)	fāteḥ	فاتح
dark (adj)	ɣāme'	غامق
bright, vivid (adj)	zāhy	زاهي
colored (pencils)	melawwen	ملوّن
color (e.g., ~ film)	melawwen	ملوّن
black-and-white (adj)	abyaḍ we aswad	أبيض وأسوّد
plain (one-colored)	sāda	سادة
multicolored (adj)	mota'added el alwān	متعددّ الألوان

11. Units of measurement

weight	wazn (m)	وزن
length	ṭūl (m)	طول

width	'arḍ (m)	عرض
height	ertefā' (m)	إرتفاع
depth	'omq (m)	عمق
volume	ḥagm (m)	حجم
area	mesāḥa (f)	مساحة
gram	gram (m)	جرام
milligram	milligrām (m)	ملّيغرام
kilogram	kilogrām (m)	كيلوغرام
ton	ṭenn (m)	طنّ
pound	reṭl (m)	رطل
ounce	onṣa (f)	أونصة
meter	metr (m)	متر
millimeter	millimetr (m)	ملّيمتر
centimeter	santimetr (m)	سنتيمتر
kilometer	kilometr (m)	كيلومتر
mile	mīl (m)	ميل
inch	boṣa (f)	بوصة
foot	'adam (m)	قدم
yard	yarda (f)	ياردة
square meter	metr morabba' (m)	متر مربّع
hectare	hektār (m)	هكتار
liter	litre (m)	لتر
degree	daraga (f)	درجة
volt	volt (m)	فولت
ampere	ambere (m)	أمبير
horsepower	ḥoṣān (m)	حصان
quantity	kemiya (f)	كميّة
a little bit of ...	ʃewayet ...	...شويّة
half	noṣṣ (m)	نصّ
dozen	desta (f)	دستة
piece (item)	waḥda (f)	وحدة
size	ḥagm (m)	حجم
scale (map ~)	me'yās (m)	مقياس
minimal (adj)	el adna	الأدنى
the smallest (adj)	el aṣɣar	الأصغر
medium (adj)	motawasseṭ	متوّسط
maximal (adj)	el aqṣa	الأقصى
the largest (adj)	el akbar	الأكبر

12. Containers

canning jar (glass ~)	barṭamān (m)	برطمان
can	kanz (m)	كانز

bucket	gardal (m)	جردل
barrel	barmīl (m)	برميل
wash basin (e.g., plastic ~)	ḥoḍe lel ɣasīl (m)	حوض للغسيل
tank (100L water ~)	χazzān (m)	خزّان
hip flask	zamzamiya (f)	زمزميّة
jerrycan	ʒerken (m)	جركن
tank (e.g., tank car)	χazzān (m)	خزّان
mug	mugg (m)	ماجّ
cup (of coffee, etc.)	fengān (m)	فنجان
saucer	ṭabaʾ fengān (m)	طبق فنجان
glass (tumbler)	kobbāya (f)	كوبّاية
wine glass	kāsa (f)	كاسة
stock pot (soup pot)	ḥalla (f)	حلّة
bottle (~ of wine)	ezāza (f)	إزازة
neck (of the bottle, etc.)	ʿonq (m)	عنق
carafe (decanter)	dawraʾ zogāgy (m)	دوّرق زجاجي
pitcher	ebrīʾ (m)	إبريق
vessel (container)	weʿāʾ (m)	وعاء
pot (crock, stoneware ~)	aṣīṣ (m)	أصيص
vase	vāza (f)	فازة
bottle (perfume ~)	ezāza (f)	إزازة
vial, small bottle	ezāza (f)	إزازة
tube (of toothpaste)	anbūba (f)	أنبوبة
sack (bag)	kīs (m)	كيس
bag (paper ~, plastic ~)	kīs (m)	كيس
pack (of cigarettes, etc.)	ʿelba (f)	علبة
box (e.g., shoebox)	ʿelba (f)	علبة
crate	ṣandūʾ (m)	صندوق
basket	salla (f)	سلّة

MAIN VERBS

T&P Books Publishing

13. The most important verbs. Part 1

to advise (vt)	naṣaḥ	نصح
to agree (say yes)	ettafa'	إتّفق
to answer (vi, vt)	gāwab	جاوب
to apologize (vi)	e'tazar	إعتذر
to arrive (vi)	weṣel	وصل
to ask (~ oneself)	sa'al	سأل
to ask (~ sb to do sth)	ṭalab	طلب
to be (vi)	kān	كان
to be afraid	χāf	خاف
to be hungry	'āyez 'ākol	عايز آكل
to be interested in ...	ehtamm be	إهتمّ بـ
to be needed	maṭlūb	مطلوب
to be surprised	etfāge'	إتفاجئ
to be thirsty	'āyez aʃrab	عايز أشرب
to begin (vt)	bada'	بدأ
to belong to ...	χaṣṣ	خصّ
to boast (vi)	tabāha	تباهى
to break (split into pieces)	kasar	كسر
to call (~ for help)	estaɣās	إستغاث
can (v aux)	'eder	قدر
to catch (vt)	mesek	مسك
to change (vt)	ɣayar	غيّر
to choose (select)	eχtār	إختار
to come down (the stairs)	nezel	نزل
to compare (vt)	qāran	قارن
to complain (vi, vt)	ʃaka	شكا
to confuse (mix up)	etlaχbaṭ	إتلخبط
to continue (vt)	wāṣel	واصل
to control (vt)	et-ḥakkem	إتحكّم
to cook (dinner)	ḥaḍḍar	حضّر
to cost (vt)	kallef	كلّف
to count (add up)	'add	عدّ
to count on ...	e'tamad 'ala ...	إعتمد على...
to create (vt)	'amal	عمل
to cry (weep)	baka	بكى

14. The most important verbs. Part 2

to deceive (vi, vt)	χadaʿ	خدع
to decorate (tree, street)	zayen	زيّن
to defend (a country, etc.)	dāfaʿ	دافع
to demand (request firmly)	ṭāleb	طالب
to dig (vt)	ḥafar	حفر
to discuss (vt)	nā'eʃ	ناقش
to do (vt)	ʿamal	عمل
to doubt (have doubts)	ʃakk fe	شكّ في
to drop (let fall)	wa''aʿ	وقّع
to enter (room, house, etc.)	daχal	دخل
to exist (vi)	kān mawgūd	كان موّجود
to expect (foresee)	tanabba'	تنبّأ
to explain (vt)	ʃaraḥ	شرح
to fall (vi)	we'eʿ	وقع
to find (vt)	la'a	لقي
to finish (vt)	χallaṣ	خلّص
to fly (vi)	ṭār	طار
to follow ... (come after)	tatabbaʿ	تتبّع
to forget (vi, vt)	nesy	نسي
to forgive (vt)	ʿafa	عفا
to give (vt)	edda	إدّى
to give a hint	edda lamḥa	إدّى لمحة
to go (on foot)	meʃy	مشى
to go for a swim	sebeḥ	سبح
to go out (for dinner, etc.)	χarag	خرج
to guess (the answer)	χammen	خمّن
to have (vt)	malak	ملك
to have breakfast	feṭer	فطر
to have dinner	etʿasʃa	إتعشّى
to have lunch	etɣadda	إتغدّى
to hear (vt)	semeʿ	سمع
to help (vt)	sāʿed	ساعد
to hide (vt)	χabba	خبّأ
to hope (vi, vt)	tamanna	تمنّى
to hunt (vi, vt)	eṣṭād	اصطاد
to hurry (vi)	estaʿgel	إستعجل

15. The most important verbs. Part 3

to inform (vt)	'āl ly	قال لي
to insist (vi, vt)	aṣarr	أصرّ

to insult (vt)	ahān	أهان
to invite (vt)	ʻazam	عزم
to joke (vi)	hazzar	هزر
to keep (vt)	ḥafaẓ	حفظ
to keep silent	seket	سكت
to kill (vt)	ʼatal	قتل
to know (sb)	ʻeref	عرف
to know (sth)	ʻeref	عرف
to laugh (vi)	ḍeḥek	ضحك
to liberate (city, etc.)	ḥarrar	حرّر
to like (I like …)	ʻagab	عجب
to look for … (search)	dawwar ʻala	دوّر على
to love (sb)	ḥabb	حب
to make a mistake	ɣeleṭ	غلط
to manage, to run	adār	أدار
to mean (signify)	ʼaṣad	قصد
to mention (talk about)	zakar	ذكر
to miss (school, etc.)	ɣāb	غاب
to notice (see)	lāḥaẓ	لاحظ
to object (vi, vt)	eʻtaraḍ	إعترض
to observe (see)	rāqab	راقب
to open (vt)	fataḥ	فتح
to order (meal, etc.)	ṭalab	طلب
to order (mil.)	amar	أمر
to own (possess)	malak	ملك
to participate (vi)	ʃārek	شارك
to pay (vi, vt)	dafaʻ	دفع
to permit (vt)	samaḥ	سمح
to plan (vt)	χaṭṭeṭ	خطّط
to play (children)	leʻeb	لعب
to pray (vi, vt)	ṣalla	صلّى
to prefer (vt)	faḍḍal	فضّل
to promise (vt)	waʻad	وعد
to pronounce (vt)	naṭaʼ	نطق
to propose (vt)	ʻaraḍ	عرض
to punish (vt)	ʻāqab	عاقب

16. The most important verbs. Part 4

to read (vi, vt)	ʼara	قرأ
to recommend (vt)	naṣaḥ	نصح
to refuse (vi, vt)	rafaḍ	رفض
to regret (be sorry)	nedem	ندم
to rent (sth from sb)	estʼgar	إستأجر

to repeat (say again)	karrar	كرّر
to reserve, to book	ḥagaz	حجز
to run (vi)	gery	جري
to save (rescue)	anqaz	أنقذ
to say (~ thank you)	'āl	قال
to scold (vt)	wabbeχ	وبّخ
to see (vt)	ʃāf	شاف
to sell (vt)	bā'	باع
to send (vt)	arsal	أرسل
to shoot (vi)	ḍarab bel nār	ضرب بالنار
to shout (vi)	ṣarraχ	صرّخ
to show (vt)	warra	ورّى
to sign (document)	waqqa'	وقّع
to sit down (vi)	'a'ad	قعد
to smile (vi)	ebtasam	إبتسم
to speak (vi, vt)	kallem	كلّم
to steal (money, etc.)	sara'	سرق
to stop (for pause, etc.)	wa''af	وقّف
to stop (please ~ calling me)	baṭṭal	بطّل
to study (vt)	daras	درس
to swim (vi)	'ām	عام
to take (vt)	aχad	أخد
to think (vi, vt)	fakkar	فكّر
to threaten (vt)	hadded	هدّد
to touch (with hands)	lamas	لمس
to translate (vt)	targem	ترجم
to trust (vt)	wasaq	وثق
to try (attempt)	ḥāwel	حاول
to turn (e.g., ~ left)	ḥād	حاد
to underestimate (vt)	estaχaff	إستخفّ
to understand (vt)	fehem	فهم
to unite (vt)	waḥḥed	وحّد
to wait (vt)	estanna	إستنّى
to want (wish, desire)	'āyez	عايز
to warn (vt)	ḥazzar	حذّر
to work (vi)	eʃtaɣal	إشتغل
to write (vt)	katab	كتب
to write down	katab	كتب

TIME. CALENDAR

T&P Books Publishing

17. Weekdays

Monday	el etneyn (m)	الإتنين
Tuesday	el talāt (m)	التلات
Wednesday	el arbeʿāʾ (m)	الأربعاء
Thursday	el χamīs (m)	الخميس
Friday	el gomʿa (m)	الجمعة
Saturday	el sabt (m)	السبت
Sunday	el aḥad (m)	الأحد
today (adv)	el naharda	النهارده
tomorrow (adv)	bokra	بكرة
the day after tomorrow	baʿd bokra (m)	بعد بكرة
yesterday (adv)	embāreḥ	امبارح
the day before yesterday	awwel embāreḥ	أوّل امبارح
day	yome (m)	يوم
working day	yome ʿamal (m)	يوم عمل
public holiday	agāza rasmiya (f)	أجازة رسميّة
day off	yome el agāza (m)	يوم أجازة
weekend	nehāyet el osbūʿ (f)	نهاية الأسبوع
all day long	ṭūl el yome	طول اليوم
the next day (adv)	fel yome elly baʿdīh	في اليوم اللي بعديه
two days ago	men yomeyn	من يومين
the day before	fel yome elly ʾablo	في اليوم اللي قبله
daily (adj)	yawmy	يومي
every day (adv)	yawmiyan	يومياً
week	osbūʿ (m)	أسبوع
last week (adv)	el esbūʿ elly fāt	الأسبوع اللي فات
next week (adv)	el esbūʿ elly gayī	الأسبوع اللي جاي
weekly (adj)	osbūʿy	أسبوعي
every week (adv)	osbūʿiyan	أسبوعياً
twice a week	marreteyn fel osbūʿ	مرّتين في الأسبوع
every Tuesday	koll solasāʾ	كلّ ثلاثاء

18. Hours. Day and night

morning	ṣobḥ (m)	صبح
in the morning	fel ṣobḥ	في الصبح
noon, midday	ẓohr (m)	ظهر
in the afternoon	baʿd el ḍohr	بعد الظهر
evening	leyl (m)	ليل

in the evening	bel leyl	بالليل
night	leyl (m)	ليل
at night	bel leyl	بالليل
midnight	noṣṣ el leyl (m)	نصّ الليل
second	sanya (f)	ثانية
minute	deʾʾa (f)	دقيقة
hour	sāʿa (f)	ساعة
half an hour	noṣṣ sāʿa (m)	نصّ ساعة
a quarter-hour	robʿ sāʿa (f)	ربع ساعة
fifteen minutes	χamastāʃer deʾʾa	خمستاشر دقيقة
24 hours	arbaʿa we ʿeʃrīn sāʿa	أربعة وعشرين ساعة
sunrise	ʃorūʾ el ʃams (m)	شروق الشمس
dawn	fagr (m)	فجر
early morning	ṣobḥ badry (m)	صبح بدري
sunset	ɣorūb el ʃams (m)	غروب الشمس
early in the morning	el ṣobḥ badry	الصبح بدري
this morning	el naharda el ṣobḥ	النهاردة الصبح
tomorrow morning	bokra el ṣobḥ	بكرة الصبح
this afternoon	el naharda baʿd el ḍohr	النهاردة بعد الظهر
in the afternoon	baʿd el ḍohr	بعد الظهر
tomorrow afternoon	bokra baʿd el ḍohr	بكرة بعد الظهر
tonight (this evening)	el naharda bel leyl	النهاردة بالليل
tomorrow night	bokra bel leyl	بكرة بالليل
at 3 o'clock sharp	es sāʿa talāta bel ḍabṭ	الساعة تلاتة بالضبط
about 4 o'clock	es sāʿa arbaʿa taʾrīban	الساعة أربعة تقريبا
by 12 o'clock	ḥatt es sāʿa etnāʃar	حتى الساعة إتناشر
in 20 minutes	fe χelāl ʿeʃrīn deʿeeʿa	في خلال عشرين دقيقة
in an hour	fe χelāl sāʿa	في خلال ساعة
on time (adv)	fe mawʿedo	في موعده
a quarter of ...	ella robʿ	إلّا ربع
within an hour	χelāl sāʿa	خلال ساعة
every 15 minutes	koll robʿ sāʿa	كلّ ربع ساعة
round the clock	leyl nahār	ليل نهار

19. Months. Seasons

January	yanāyer (m)	يناير
February	febrāyer (m)	فبراير
March	māres (m)	مارس
April	ebrīl (m)	إبريل
May	māyo (m)	مايو
June	yonyo (m)	يونيو
July	yolyo (m)	يوليو

August	oɣosṭos (m)	أغسطس
September	sebtamber (m)	سبتمبر
October	oktober (m)	أكتوبر
November	november (m)	نوفمبر
December	desember (m)	ديسمبر
spring	rabee‘ (m)	ربيع
in spring	fel rabee‘	في الربيع
spring (as adj)	rabee‘y	ربيعي
summer	ṣeyf (m)	صيف
in summer	fel ṣeyf	في الصيف
summer (as adj)	ṣeyfy	صيفي
fall	χarīf (m)	خريف
in fall	fel χarīf	في الخريف
fall (as adj)	χarīfy	خريفي
winter	ʃetā’ (m)	شتاء
in winter	fel ʃetā’	في الشتاء
winter (as adj)	ʃetwy	شتوّي
month	ʃahr (m)	شهر
this month	fel ʃahr da	في الشهر ده
next month	el ʃahr el gayī	الشهر الجايّ
last month	el ʃahr elly fāt	الشهر اللي فات
a month ago	men ʃahr	من شهر
in a month (a month later)	ba‘d ʃahr	بعد شهر
in 2 months (2 months later)	ba‘d ʃahreyn	بعد شهرين
the whole month	el ʃahr kollo	الشهر كلّه
all month long	ṭawāl el ʃahr	طوال الشهر
monthly (~ magazine)	ʃahry	شهري
monthly (adv)	ʃahry	شهري
every month	koll ʃahr	كلّ شهر
twice a month	marreteyn fel ʃahr	مرّتين في الشهر
year	sana (f)	سنة
this year	el sana di	السنة دي
next year	el sana el gaya	السنة الجايّة
last year	el sana elly fātet	السنة اللي فاتت
a year ago	men sana	من سنة
in a year	ba‘d sana	بعد سنة
in two years	ba‘d sanateyn	بعد سنتين
the whole year	el sana kollaha	السنة كلّها
all year long	ṭūl el sana	طول السنة
every year	koll sana	كلّ سنة
annual (adj)	sanawy	سنوّي

annually (adv)	koll sana	كلّ سنة
4 times a year	arbaʿ marrāt fel sana	أربع مرات في السنة
date (e.g., today's ~)	tarīχ (m)	تاريخ
date (e.g., ~ of birth)	tarīχ (m)	تاريخ
calendar	natīga (f)	نتيجة
half a year	noṣṣ sana	نصّ سنة
six months	settet aʃ-hor (f)	ستّة أشهر
season (summer, etc.)	faṣl (m)	فصل
century	qarn (m)	قرن

TRAVEL. HOTEL

T&P Books Publishing

20. Trip. Travel

tourism, travel	seyāḥa (f)	سياحة
tourist	sā'eḥ (m)	سائح
trip, voyage	reḥla (f)	رحلة
adventure	moɣamra (f)	مغامرة
trip, journey	reḥla (f)	رحلة
vacation	agāza (f)	أجازة
to be on vacation	kān fi agāza	كان في أجازة
rest	estrāḥa (f)	إستراحة
train	qeṭār, 'aṭṭr (m)	قطار
by train	bel qeṭār - bel aṭṭr	بالقطار
airplane	ṭayāra (f)	طيّارة
by airplane	bel ṭayāra	بالطيّارة
by car	bel sayāra	بالسيّارة
by ship	bel safīna	بالسفينة
luggage	el ʃonaṭ (pl)	الشنط
suitcase	ʃanṭa (f)	شنطة
luggage cart	'arabet ʃonaṭ (f)	عربة شنط
passport	basbore (m)	باسبور
visa	ta'ʃīra (f)	تأشيرة
ticket	tazkara (f)	تذكرة
air ticket	tazkara ṭayarān (f)	تذكرة طيران
guidebook	dalīl (m)	دليل
map (tourist ~)	χarīṭa (f)	خريطة
area (rural ~)	mante'a (f)	منطقة
place, site	makān (m)	مكان
exotica (n)	ɣarāba (f)	غرابة
exotic (adj)	ɣarīb	غريب
amazing (adj)	mod-heʃ	مدهش
group	magmū'a (f)	مجموعة
excursion, sightseeing tour	gawla (f)	جولة
guide (person)	morʃed (m)	مرشد

21. Hotel

hotel	fondo' (m)	فندق
motel	motel (m)	موتيل

three-star (~ hotel)	talat nogūm	ثلاث نجوم
five-star	χamas nogūm	خمس نجوم
to stay (in a hotel, etc.)	nezel	نزل
room	oḍa (f)	أوضة
single room	owḍa le ʃaχṣ wāḥed (f)	أوضة لشخص واحد
double room	oḍa le ʃaχṣeyn (f)	أوضة لشخصين
to book a room	ḥagaz owḍa	حجز أوضة
half board	wagbeteyn fel yome (du)	وجبتين في اليوم
full board	talat wagabāt fel yome	ثلاث وجبات في اليوم
with bath	bel banyo	بـ البانيو
with shower	bel doʃ	بالدوش
satellite television	televizion be qanawāt faḍā'iya (m)	تليفزيون بقنوات فضائية
air-conditioner	takyīf (m)	تكييف
towel	fūṭa (f)	فوطة
key	meftāḥ (m)	مفتاح
administrator	modīr (m)	مدير
chambermaid	'āmela tandīf γoraf (f)	عاملة تنظيف غرف
porter, bellboy	ʃayāl (m)	شيّال
doorman	bawwāb (m)	بوّاب
restaurant	maṭ'am (m)	مطعم
pub, bar	bār (m)	بار
breakfast	foṭūr (m)	فطور
dinner	'aʃā' (m)	عشاء
buffet	bofeyh (m)	بوفيه
lobby	rad-ha (f)	ردهة
elevator	asanseyr (m)	اسانسير
DO NOT DISTURB	nargu 'adam el ez'āg	نرجو عدم الإزعاج
NO SMOKING	mamnū' el tadχīn	ممنوع التدخين

22. Sightseeing

monument	temsāl (m)	تمثال
fortress	'al'a (f)	قلعة
palace	'aṣr (m)	قصر
castle	'al'a (f)	قلعة
tower	borg (m)	برج
mausoleum	ḍarīḥ (m)	ضريح
architecture	handasa me'māriya (f)	هندسة معمارية
medieval (adj)	men el qorūn el wosṭa	من القرون الوسطى
ancient (adj)	'atīq	عتيق
national (adj)	waṭany	وطني

famous (monument, etc.)	maʃ-hūr	مشهور
tourist	sā'eḥ (m)	سائح
guide (person)	morʃed (m)	مرشد
excursion, sightseeing tour	gawla (f)	جولة
to show (vt)	warra	ورّى
to tell (vt)	'āl	قال
to find (vt)	la'a	لقى
to get lost (lose one's way)	ḍā'	ضاع
map (e.g., subway ~)	χarīṭa (f)	خريطة
map (e.g., city ~)	χarīṭa (f)	خريطة
souvenir, gift	tezkār (m)	تذكار
gift shop	maḥal hadāya (m)	محل هدايا
to take pictures	ṣawwar	صوّر
to have one's picture taken	etṣawwar	إتصوّر

TRANSPORTATION

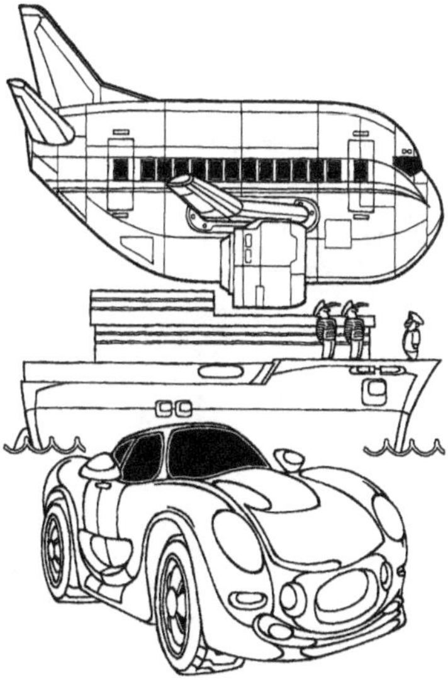

T&P Books Publishing

23. Airport

airport	maṭār (m)	مطار
airplane	ṭayāra (f)	طيّارة
airline	ʃerket ṭayarān (f)	شركة طيران
air traffic controller	marākeb el ḥaraka el gawiya (m)	مراكب الحركة الجويّة
departure	moɣadra (f)	مغادرة
arrival	woṣūl (m)	وصول
to arrive (by plane)	weṣel	وصل
departure time	wa'ʾt el moɣadra (m)	وقت المغادرة
arrival time	wa'ʾt el woṣūl (m)	وقت الوصول
to be delayed	ta'ʾakχar	تأخّر
flight delay	ta'ʾaχor el reḥla (m)	تأخّر الرحلة
information board	lawḥet el maʿlomāt (f)	لوحة المعلومات
information	esteʿlamāt (pl)	إستعلامات
to announce (vt)	aʿlan	أعلن
flight (e.g., next ~)	reḥlet ṭayarān (f)	رحلة طيران
customs	gamārek (pl)	جمارك
customs officer	mowazzaf el gamārek (m)	موظّف الجمارك
customs declaration	taṣrīḥ gomroky (m)	تصريح جمركي
to fill out (vt)	mala	ملا
to fill out the declaration	mala el taṣrīḥ	ملأ التصريح
passport control	taftīʃ el gawazāt (m)	تفتيش الجوازات
luggage	el ʃonaṭ (pl)	الشنط
hand luggage	ʃonaṭ el yad (pl)	شنط اليد
luggage cart	ʿarabet ʃonaṭ (f)	عربة شنط
landing	hobūṭ (m)	هبوط
landing strip	mamarr el hobūṭ (m)	ممرّ الهبوط
to land (vi)	habaṭ	هبط
airstairs	sellem el ṭayāra (m)	سلّم الطيّارة
check-in	tasgīl (m)	تسجيل
check-in counter	makān tasgīl (m)	مكان تسجيل
to check-in (vi)	saggel	سجّل
boarding pass	beṭāqet el rokūb (f)	بطاقة الركوب
departure gate	bawwābet el moɣadra (f)	بوّابة المغادرة
transit	tranzīt (m)	ترانزيت

to wait (vt)	estanna	إستنّى
departure lounge	ṣālet el moɣadra (f)	صالة المغادرة
to see off	wadda'	ودّع
to say goodbye	wadda'	ودّع

24. Airplane

airplane	ṭayāra (f)	طيّارة
air ticket	tazkara ṭayarān (f)	تذكرة طيران
airline	ʃerket ṭayarān (f)	شركة طيران
airport	maṭār (m)	مطار
supersonic (adj)	χāreq lel ṣote	خارق للصوت
captain	kabten (m)	كابتن
crew	ṭa'm (m)	طقم
pilot	ṭayār (m)	طيّار
flight attendant (fem.)	moḍīfet ṭayarān (f)	مضيفة طيران
navigator	mallāḥ (m)	ملّاح
wings	agneḥa (pl)	أجنحة
tail	deyl (m)	ذيل
cockpit	kabīna (f)	كابينة
engine	motore (m)	موتور
undercarriage (landing gear)	'agalāt el hobūṭ (pl)	عجلات الهبوط
turbine	torbīna (f)	توربينة
propeller	marwaḥa (f)	مروّحة
black box	mosaggel el ṭayarān (m)	مسجّل الطيران
yoke (control column)	moqawwed el ṭayāra (m)	مقوّد الطيّارة
fuel	woqūd (m)	وقود
safety card	beṭā'et el salāma (f)	بطاقة السلامة
oxygen mask	mask el oksyʒīn (m)	ماسك الاوكسيجين
uniform	zayī muwaḥḥad (m)	زيّ موحّد
life vest	sotret nagah (f)	سترة نجاة
parachute	baraʃot (m)	باراشوت
takeoff	eqlā' (m)	إقلاع
to take off (vi)	aqla'et	أقلعت
runway	modarrag el ṭa'erāṭ (m)	مدرّج الطائرات
visibility	ro'ya (f)	رؤية
flight (act of flying)	ṭayarān (m)	طيران
altitude	ertefā' (m)	إرتفاع
air pocket	geyb hawā'y (m)	جيب هوائي
seat	meq'ad (m)	مقعد
headphones	samma'āt ra'siya (pl)	سمّاعات رأسية
folding tray (tray table)	ṣeniya qabela lel ṭayī (f)	صينية قابلة للطيّ

airplane window	ʃebbāk el ṭayāra (m)	شبّاك الطيّارة
aisle	mamarr (m)	ممرّ

25. Train

train	qeṭār, 'aṭṭr (m)	قطار
commuter train	qeṭār rokkāb (m)	قطار ركّاب
express train	qeṭār saree' (m)	قطار سريع
diesel locomotive	qāṭeret dīzel (f)	قاطرة ديزل
steam locomotive	qāṭera boχariya (f)	قاطرة بخاريّة
passenger car	'araba (f)	عربة
dining car	'arabet el ṭa'ām (f)	عربة الطعام
rails	qoḍbān (pl)	قضبان
railroad	sekka ḥadīdiya (f)	سكّة حديديّة
railway tie	'āreḍa sekket ḥadīd (f)	عارضة سكّة الحديد
platform (railway ~)	raṣīf (m)	رصيف
track (~ 1, 2, etc.)	χaṭṭ (m)	خطّ
semaphore	semafore (m)	سيمافور
station	maḥaṭṭa (f)	محطّة
engineer (train driver)	sawwā' (m)	سوّاق
porter (of luggage)	ʃayāl (m)	شيّال
car attendant	mas'ūl 'arabet el qeṭār (m)	مسؤول عربة القطار
passenger	rākeb (m)	راكب
conductor (ticket inspector)	kamsary (m)	كمسري
corridor (in train)	mamarr (m)	ممرّ
emergency brake	farāmel el ṭawāre' (pl)	فرامل الطوارئ
compartment	ɣorfa (f)	غرفة
berth	serīr (m)	سرير
upper berth	serīr 'olwy (m)	سرير علوّي
lower berth	serīr sofly (m)	سرير سفلي
bed linen, bedding	aɣṭeyet el serīr (pl)	أغطية السرير
ticket	tazkara (f)	تذكرة
schedule	gadwal (m)	جدول
information display	lawḥet ma'lomāt (f)	لوحة معلومات
to leave, to depart	ɣādar	غادر
departure (of train)	moɣadra (f)	مغادرة
to arrive (ab. train)	weṣel	وصل
arrival	woṣūl (m)	وصول
to arrive by train	weṣel bel qeṭār	وصل بالقطار
to get on the train	rekeb el qeṭār	ركب القطار

to get off the train	nezel men el qeṭār	نزل من القطار
train wreck	ḥeṭām qeṭār (m)	حطام قطار
to derail (vi)	χarag ʿan χaṭṭ sīru	خرج عن خطّ سيره
steam locomotive	qāṭera boχariya (f)	قاطرة بخاريّة
stoker, fireman	ʿatʃagy (m)	عطشجي
firebox	forn el moḥarrek (m)	فرن المحرّك
coal	faḥm (m)	فحم

26. Ship

ship	safīna (f)	سفينة
vessel	safīna (f)	سفينة
steamship	baχera (f)	باخرة
riverboat	baχera nahriya (f)	باخرة نهرية
cruise ship	safīna seyaḥiya (f)	سفينة سياحيّة
cruiser	ṭarrād safīna baḥariya (m)	طرّاد سفينة بحريّة
yacht	yaχt (m)	يخت
tugboat	qāṭera baḥariya (f)	قاطرة بحريّة
barge	ṣandal (m)	صندل
ferry	ʿabbāra (f)	عبّارة
sailing ship	safīna ʃeraʿiya (m)	سفينة شراعيّة
brigantine	markeb ʃerāʿy (m)	مركب شراعي
ice breaker	moḥaṭṭemet galīd (f)	محطّمة جليد
submarine	ɣawwāṣa (f)	غوّاصة
boat (flat-bottomed ~)	markeb (m)	مركب
dinghy	zawraʾ (m)	زورق
lifeboat	qāreb nagah (m)	قارب نجاة
motorboat	lunʃ (m)	لنش
captain	ʾobṭān (m)	قبطان
seaman	baḥḥār (m)	بحّار
sailor	baḥḥār (m)	بحّار
crew	ṭāqem (m)	طاقم
boatswain	rabbān (m)	ربّان
ship's boy	ṣaby el safīna (m)	صبي السفينة
cook	ṭabbāχ (m)	طبّاخ
ship's doctor	ṭabīb el safīna (m)	طبيب السفينة
deck	saṭ-ḥ el safīna (m)	سطح السفينة
mast	sāreya (f)	سارية
sail	ʃerāʿ (m)	شراع
hold	ʿanbar (m)	عنبر
bow (prow)	moʾaddema (m)	مقدّمة

stern	mo'aχeret el safīna (f)	مؤخّرة السفينة
oar	megdāf (m)	مجذاف
screw propeller	marwaḥa (f)	مروّحة
cabin	kabīna (f)	كابينة
wardroom	ɣorfet el ṭa'ām wel rāḥa (f)	غرفة الطعام والراحة
engine room	qesm el 'ālāt (m)	قسم الآلات
bridge	borg el qeyāda (m)	برج القيادة
radio room	ɣorfet el lāselky (f)	غرفة اللاسلكي
wave (radio)	mouga (f)	موجة
logbook	segel el safīna (m)	سجل السفينة
spyglass	monzār (m)	منظار
bell	garas (m)	جرس
flag	'alam (m)	علم
hawser (mooring ~)	ḥabl (m)	حبل
knot (bowline, etc.)	'o'da (f)	عقدة
deckrails	drabzīn saṭ-ḥ el safīna (m)	درابزين سطح السفينة
gangway	sellem (m)	سلّم
anchor	marsāh (f)	مرساة
to weigh anchor	rafa' morsah	رفع مرساة
to drop anchor	rasa	رسا
anchor chain	selselet morsah (f)	سلسلة مرساة
port (harbor)	minā' (m)	ميناء
quay, wharf	marsa (m)	مرسى
to berth (moor)	rasa	رسا
to cast off	aqla'	أقلع
trip, voyage	reḥla (f)	رحلة
cruise (sea trip)	reḥla baḥariya (f)	رحلة بحريّة
course (route)	masār (m)	مسار
route (itinerary)	ṭarī' (m)	طريق
fairway (safe water channel)	magra melāḥy (m)	مجرى ملاحيّ
shallows	meyāh ḍaḥla (f)	مياه ضحلة
to run aground	ganaḥ	جنح
storm	'āṣefa (f)	عاصفة
signal	eʃara (f)	إشارة
to sink (vi)	ɣere'	غرق
Man overboard!	sa'aṭ rāgil min el sefīna!	!سقط راجل من السفينة
SOS (distress signal)	nedā' eɣāsa (m)	نداء إغاثة
ring buoy	ṭo'e nagah (m)	طوق نجاة

CITY

T&P Books Publishing

27. Urban transportation

bus	buṣ (m)	باص
streetcar	trām (m)	ترام
trolley bus	trolly buṣ (m)	ترولي باص
route (of bus, etc.)	χaṭṭ (m)	خطّ
number (e.g., bus ~)	raqam (m)	رقم
to go by ...	rāḥ be ...	راح بـ ...
to get on (~ the bus)	rekeb	ركب
to get off ...	nezel men	نزل من
stop (e.g., bus ~)	maw'af (m)	موّقف
next stop	el maḥaṭṭa el gaya (f)	المحطة الجايّة
terminus	'āχer maw'af (m)	آخر موقف
schedule	gadwal (m)	جدوَل
to wait (vt)	estanna	إستنّى
ticket	tazkara (f)	تذكرة
fare	ogra (f)	أجرة
cashier (ticket seller)	kaʃier (m)	كاشيير
ticket inspection	taftīʃ el tazāker (m)	تفتيش التذاكر
ticket inspector	mofatteʃ tazāker (m)	مفتّش تذاكر
to be late (for ...)	met'akχer	متأخّر
to miss (~ the train, etc.)	ta'akχar	تأخّر
to be in a hurry	mesta'gel	مستعجل
taxi, cab	taksi (m)	تاكسي
taxi driver	sawwā' taksi (m)	سوّاق تاكسي
by taxi	bel taksi	بالتاكسي
taxi stand	maw'ef taksi (m)	موّقف تاكسي
to call a taxi	kallem taksi	كلّم تاكسي
to take a taxi	aχad taksi	أخد تاكسي
traffic	ḥaraket el morūr (f)	حركة المرور
traffic jam	zaḥmet el morūr (f)	زحمة المرور
rush hour	sā'et el zorwa (f)	ساعة الذروة
to park (vi)	rakan	ركن
to park (vt)	rakan	ركن
parking lot	maw'ef el 'arabeyāt (m)	موقف العربيات
subway	metro (m)	مترو
station	maḥaṭṭa (f)	محطّة
to take the subway	aχad el metro	أخد المترو

train	qeṭār, 'aṭṭr (m)	قطار
train station	maḥaṭṭet qeṭār (f)	محطّة قطار

28. City. Life in the city

city, town	madīna (f)	مدينة
capital city	'āṣema (f)	عاصمة
village	qarya (f)	قرية
city map	xarīṭet el madinah (f)	خريطة المدينة
downtown	wesṭ el balad (m)	وسط البلد
suburb	ḍāḥeya (f)	ضاحية
suburban (adj)	el ḍawāḥy	الضواحي
outskirts	aṭrāf el madīna (pl)	أطراف المدينة
environs (suburbs)	ḍawāḥy el madīna (pl)	ضواحي المدينة
city block	ḥayī (m)	حي
residential block (area)	ḥayī sakany (m)	حي سكني
traffic	ḥaraket el morūr (f)	حركة المرور
traffic lights	eʃārāt el morūr (pl)	إشارات المرور
public transportation	wasā'el el na'l (pl)	وسائل النقل
intersection	taqāṭo' (m)	تقاطع
crosswalk	ma'bar (m)	معبر
pedestrian underpass	nafa' moʃāh (m)	نفق مشاه
to cross (~ the street)	'abar	عبر
pedestrian	māʃy (m)	ماشي
sidewalk	raṣīf (m)	رصيف
bridge	kobry (m)	كبري
embankment (river walk)	korneyʃ (m)	كورنيش
fountain	nafūra (f)	نافورة
allée (garden walkway)	mamʃa (m)	ممشى
park	ḥadīqa (f)	حديقة
boulevard	bolvār (m)	بولفار
square	medān (m)	ميدان
avenue (wide street)	ʃāre' (m)	شارع
street	ʃāre' (m)	شارع
side street	zo'ā' (m)	زقاق
dead end	ṭarī' masdūd (m)	طريق مسدود
house	beyt (m)	بيت
building	mabna (m)	مبنى
skyscraper	nāṭeḥet sahāb (f)	ناطحة سحاب
facade	waɣa (f)	واجهة
roof	sa'f (m)	سقف
window	ʃebbāk (m)	شبّاك

arch	qose (m)	قوس
column	ʿamūd (m)	عمود
corner	zawya (f)	زاوية
store window	vatrīna (f)	فترينة
signboard (store sign, etc.)	yafṭa, lāfeta (f)	لافتة, يافطة
poster	boster (m)	بوستر
advertising poster	boster eʿlān (m)	بوستر إعلان
billboard	lawḥet eʿlanāt (f)	لوحة إعلانات
garbage, trash	zebāla (f)	زبالة
trashcan (public ~)	ṣandūʾ zebāla (m)	صندوق زبالة
to litter (vi)	rama zebāla	رمى زبالة
garbage dump	mazbala (f)	مزبلة
phone booth	koʃk telefōn (m)	كشك تليفون
lamppost	ʿamūd nūr (m)	عمود نور
bench (park ~)	korsy (m)	كرسي
police officer	ʃorṭy (m)	شرطي
police	ʃorṭa (f)	شرطة
beggar	ʃaḥḥāt (m)	شحّات
homeless (n)	motaʃarred (m)	متشرّد

29. Urban institutions

store	maḥal (m)	محل
drugstore, pharmacy	ṣaydaliya (f)	صيدليّة
eyeglass store	maḥal naḍḍārāt (m)	محل نضّارات
shopping mall	mole (m)	مول
supermarket	subermarket (m)	سوبرماركت
bakery	maχbaz (m)	مخبز
baker	χabbāz (m)	خبّاز
pastry shop	ḥalawāny (m)	حلواني
grocery store	baʾʾāla (f)	بقّالة
butcher shop	gezāra (f)	جزارة
produce store	dokkān χoḍār (m)	دكّان خضار
market	sūʾ (f)	سوق
coffee house	ʾahwa (f), kaféih (m)	قهوة ,كافيه
restaurant	maṭʿam (m)	مطعم
pub, bar	bār (m)	بار
pizzeria	maḥal pizza (m)	محل بيتزا
hair salon	ṣalone ḥelāʾa (m)	صالون حلاقة
post office	maktab el barīd (m)	مكتب البريد
dry cleaners	dray klīn (m)	دراي كلين
photo studio	estudio taṣwīr (m)	إستوديو تصوير

shoe store	maḥal gezam (m)	محل جزم
bookstore	maḥal kotob (m)	محل كتب
sporting goods store	maḥal mostalzamāt reyaḍiya (m)	محل مستلزمات رياضية
clothes repair shop	maḥal χeyāṭet malābes (m)	محل خياطة ملابس
formal wear rental	ta'gīr malābes rasmiya (m)	تأجير ملابس رسمية
video rental store	maḥal ta'gīr video (m)	محل تأجير فيديو
circus	serk (m)	سيرك
zoo	ḥadīqet el ḥayawān (f)	حديقة حيوان
movie theater	sinema (f)	سينما
museum	mat-ḥaf (m)	متحف
library	maktaba (f)	مكتبة
theater	masraḥ (m)	مسرح
opera (opera house)	obra (f)	أوبرا
nightclub	malha leyly (m)	ملهى ليّلي
casino	kazino (m)	كازينو
mosque	masged (m)	مسجد
synagogue	kenīs (m)	كنيس
cathedral	katedra'iya (f)	كاتدرائية
temple	ma'bad (m)	معبد
church	kenīsa (f)	كنيسة
college	kolliya (m)	كليّة
university	gam'a (f)	جامعة
school	madrasa (f)	مدرسة
prefecture	moqaṭ'a (f)	مقاطعة
city hall	baladiya (f)	بلديّة
hotel	fondo' (m)	فندق
bank	bank (m)	بنك
embassy	safāra (f)	سفارة
travel agency	ʃerket seyāḥa (f)	شركة سياحة
information office	maktab el este'lāmāt (m)	مكتب الإستعلامات
currency exchange	ṣarrāfa (f)	صرّافة
subway	metro (m)	مترو
hospital	mostaʃfa (m)	مستشفى
gas station	maḥaṭṭet banzīn (f)	محطّة بنزين
parking lot	maw'ef el 'arabeyāt (m)	موقف العربيات

30. Signs

signboard (store sign, etc.)	yafṭa, lāfeta (f)	لافتة, يافطة
notice (door sign, etc.)	bayān (m)	بيان

poster	boster (m)	بوستر
direction sign	'alāmet (f)	علامة إتجاه
arrow (sign)	'alāmet eʃāra (f)	علامة إشارة
caution	taḥzīr (m)	تحذير
warning sign	lāfetat taḥzīr (f)	لافتة تحذير
to warn (vt)	ḥazzar	حذّر
rest day (weekly ~)	yome 'oṭla (m)	يوم عطلة
timetable (schedule)	gadwal (m)	جدوَل
opening hours	aw'āt el 'amal (pl)	أوقات العمل
WELCOME!	ahlan w sahlan!	أهلاً وسهلا!
ENTRANCE	doχūl	دخول
EXIT	χorūg	خروج
PUSH	edfa'	إدفع
PULL	es-ḥab	إسحب
OPEN	maftūḥ	مفتوح
CLOSED	moɣlaq	مغلق
WOMEN	lel sayedāt	للسيدات
MEN	lel regāl	للرجال
DISCOUNTS	χoṣomāt	خصومات
SALE	taχfeḍāt	تخفيضات
NEW!	gedīd!	جديد!
FREE	maggānan	مجّاناً
ATTENTION!	entebāh!	إنتباه!
NO VACANCIES	koll el amāken maḥgūza	كلّ الأماكن محجوزة
RESERVED	maḥgūz	محجوز
ADMINISTRATION	edāra	إدارة
STAFF ONLY	lel 'amelīn faqaṭ	للعاملين فقط
BEWARE OF THE DOG!	eḥzar wogūd kalb	إحذر وجود الكلب
NO SMOKING	mamnū' el tadχīn	ممنوع التدخين
DO NOT TOUCH!	'adam el lams	عدم اللمس
DANGEROUS	χaṭīr	خطير
DANGER	χaṭar	خطر
HIGH VOLTAGE	tayār 'āly	تيّار عالي
NO SWIMMING!	el sebāḥa mamnū'a	السباحة ممنوعة
OUT OF ORDER	mo'aṭṭal	معطّل
FLAMMABLE	saree' el eʃte'āl	سريع الإشتعال
FORBIDDEN	mamnū'	ممنوع
NO TRESPASSING!	mamnū' el morūr	ممنوع المرور
WET PAINT	eḥzar ṭelā' ɣayr gāf	احذر طلاء غير جاف

31. Shopping

to buy (purchase)	eʃtara	إشترى
purchase	ḥāga (f)	حاجة
to go shopping	eʃtara	إشترى
shopping	ʃobbing (m)	شوبينج
to be open (ab. store)	maftūḥ	مفتوح
to be closed	moɣlaq	مغلق
footwear, shoes	gezam (pl)	جزم
clothes, clothing	malābes (pl)	ملابس
cosmetics	mawād tagmīl (pl)	مواد تجميل
food products	akl (m)	أكل
gift, present	hediya (f)	هديّة
salesman	bayā' (m)	بيّاع
saleswoman	bayā'a (f)	بيّاعة
check out, cash desk	ṣandū' el daf' (m)	صندوق الدفع
mirror	merāya (f)	مراية
counter (store ~)	manḍada (f)	منضدة
fitting room	ɣorfet el 'eyās (f)	غرفة القياس
to try on	garrab	جرّب
to fit (ab. dress, etc.)	nāseb	ناسب
to like (I like ...)	'agab	عجب
price	se'r (m)	سعر
price tag	tiket el se'r (m)	تيكت السعر
to cost (vt)	kallef	كلّف
How much?	bekām?	بكام؟
discount	χaṣm (m)	خصم
inexpensive (adj)	meʃ ɣāly	مش غالي
cheap (adj)	reχīṣ	رخيص
expensive (adj)	ɣāly	غالي
It's expensive	da ɣāly	ده غالي
rental (n)	este'gār (m)	إستئجار
to rent (~ a tuxedo)	est'gar	إستأجر
credit (trade credit)	e'temān (m)	إئتمان
on credit (adv)	bel ta'seeṭ	بالتقسيط

CLOTHING & ACCESSORIES

T&P Books Publishing

32. Outerwear. Coats

clothes	malābes (pl)	ملابس
outerwear	malābes fo'aniya (pl)	ملابس فوقانيّة
winter clothing	malābes ʃetwiya (pl)	ملابس شتويّة
coat (overcoat)	balṭo (m)	بالطو
fur coat	balṭo farww (m)	بالطو فروّ
fur jacket	ʒaket farww (m)	جاكيت فروّ
down coat	balṭo maḥʃy rīʃ (m)	بالطو محشي ريش
jacket (e.g., leather ~)	ʒæket (m)	جاكيت
raincoat (trenchcoat, etc.)	ʒæket lel maṭar (m)	جاكيت للمطر
waterproof (adj)	wāqy men el maya	واقي من الميّة

33. Men's & women's clothing

shirt (button shirt)	'amīṣ (m)	قميص
pants	banṭalone (f)	بنطلون
jeans	ʒeans (m)	جينز
suit jacket	ʒæket (f)	جاكت
suit	badla (f)	بدلة
dress (frock)	fostān (m)	فستان
skirt	ʒība (f)	جيبة
blouse	bloza (f)	بلوزة
knitted jacket (cardigan, etc.)	kardigan (m)	كارديجن
jacket (of woman's suit)	ʒæket (m)	جاكيت
T-shirt	ti ʃirt (m)	تي شيرت
shorts (short trousers)	ʃort (m)	شورت
tracksuit	treneng (m)	تريننج
bathrobe	robe el ḥammām (m)	روب حمّام
pajamas	beʒāma (f)	بيجاما
sweater	blover (f)	بلوفر
pullover	blover (m)	بلوفر
vest	vest (m)	فيست
tailcoat	badlet sahra ṭawīla (f)	بدلة سهرة طويلة
tuxedo	badla (f)	بدلة
uniform	zayī muwaḥḥad (m)	زيّ موحّد
workwear	lebs el ʃoɣl (m)	لبس الشغل

overalls	overall (m)	اوفر اول
coat (e.g., doctor's smock)	balṭo (m)	بالطو

34. Clothing. Underwear

underwear	malābes dāχeliya (pl)	ملابس داخلية
boxers, briefs	sirwāl dāχly rigāly (m)	سروال داخلي رجاليّ
panties	sirwāl dāχly nisā'y (m)	سروال داخلي نسائي
undershirt (A-shirt)	fanella (f)	فانلّا
socks	ʃarāb (m)	شراب
nightgown	'amīṣ nome (m)	قميص نوم
bra	setyāna (f)	ستيانة
knee highs (knee-high socks)	ʃarabāt ṭawīla (pl)	شرابات طويلة
pantyhose	klone (m)	كلون
stockings (thigh highs)	gawāreb (pl)	جوارب
bathing suit	mayo (m)	مايّوه

35. Headwear

hat	ṭa'iya (f)	طاقيّة
fedora	borneyṭa (f)	برنيطة
baseball cap	base bāl kāb (m)	بيس بول كاب
flatcap	ṭa'iya mosaṭṭaḥa (f)	طاقيّة مسطحة
beret	bereyh (m)	بيريه
hood	ɣaṭa' (f)	غطاء
panama hat	qobba'et banama (f)	قبّعة بناما
knit cap (knitted hat)	ays kāb (m)	آيس كاب
headscarf	eʃarb (m)	إيشارب
women's hat	borneyṭa (f)	برنيطة
hard hat	χawza (f)	خوذة
garrison cap	kāb (m)	كاب
helmet	χawza (f)	خوذة
derby	qobba'a (f)	قبّعة
top hat	qobba'a rasmiya (f)	قبّعة رسمية

36. Footwear

footwear	gezam (pl)	جزم
shoes (men's shoes)	gazma (f)	جزمة
shoes (women's shoes)	gazma (f)	جزمة

boots (e.g., cowboy ~)	būt (m)	بوت
slippers	ʃebʃeb (m)	شبشب
tennis shoes (e.g., Nike ~)	kotʃy tennis (m)	كوتشي تنس
sneakers (e.g., Converse ~)	kotʃy (m)	كوتشي
sandals	ṣandal (pl)	صندل
cobbler (shoe repairer)	eskāfy (m)	إسكافي
heel	ka'b (m)	كعب
pair (of shoes)	goze (m)	جوز
shoestring	ʃerī'ṭ (m)	شريط
to lace (vt)	rabaṭ	ربط
shoehorn	labbāsa el gazma (f)	لبّاسة الجزمة
shoe polish	warnīʃ el gazma (m)	ورنيش الجزمة

37. Personal accessories

gloves	gwanty (m)	جوانتي
mittens	gwanty men ɣeyr aṣābe' (m)	جوانتي من غير أصابع
scarf (muffler)	skarf (m)	سكارف
glasses (eyeglasses)	naḍḍāra (f)	نظّارة
frame (eyeglass ~)	eṭār (m)	إطار
umbrella	ʃamsiya (f)	شمسيّة
walking stick	'aṣāya (f)	عصاية
hairbrush	forʃet ʃa'r (f)	فرشة شعر
fan	marwaḥa (f)	مروّحة
tie (necktie)	karavetta (f)	كرافتة
bow tie	bebyona (m)	بيبيونة
suspenders	ḥammala (f)	حمّالة
handkerchief	mandīl (m)	منديل
comb	meʃṭ (m)	مشط
barrette	dabbūs (m)	دبّوس
hairpin	bensa (m)	بنسة
buckle	bokla (f)	بكلة
belt	ḥezām (m)	حزام
shoulder strap	ḥammalet el ketf (f)	حمّالة الكتف
bag (handbag)	ʃanṭa (f)	شنطة
purse	ʃanṭet yad (f)	شنطة يد
backpack	ʃanṭet ḍahr (f)	شنطة ظهر

38. Clothing. Miscellaneous

fashion	mūḍa (f)	موضة
in vogue (adj)	fel moḍa	في الموضة
fashion designer	moṣammem azyā' (m)	مصمّم أزياء
collar	yā'a (f)	ياقة
pocket	geyb (m)	جيب
pocket (as adj)	geyb	جيب
sleeve	komm (m)	كمّ
hanging loop	'elāqa (f)	علّاقة
fly (on trousers)	lesān (m)	لسان
zipper (fastener)	sosta (f)	سوستة
fastener	maʃbak (m)	مشبك
button	zerr (m)	زرّ
buttonhole	'arwa (f)	عروة
to come off (ab. button)	we'e'	وقع
to sew (vi, vt)	χayaṭ	خيّط
to embroider (vi, vt)	ṭarraz	طرّز
embroidery	taṭrīz (m)	تطريز
sewing needle	ebra (f)	إبرة
thread	χeyṭ (m)	خيط
seam	derz (m)	درز
to get dirty (vi)	ettwassaχ	إتّوسّخ
stain (mark, spot)	bo''a (f)	بقعة
to crease, crumple (vi)	takarmaʃ	تكرمش
to tear, to rip (vt)	'aṭa'	قطع
clothes moth	'etta (f)	عتّة

39. Personal care. Cosmetics

toothpaste	ma'gūn asnān (m)	معجون أسنان
toothbrush	forʃet senān (f)	فرشة أسنان
to brush one's teeth	naḍḍaf el asnān	نظّف الأسنان
razor	mūs (m)	موس
shaving cream	krīm ḥelā'a (m)	كريم حلاقة
to shave (vi)	ḥala'	حلق
soap	ṣabūn (m)	صابون
shampoo	ʃambū (m)	شامبو
scissors	ma'aṣ (m)	مقص
nail file	mabrad (m)	مبرد
nail clippers	mel'aṭ (m)	ملقط
tweezers	mel'aṭ (m)	ملقط

cosmetics	mawād tagmīl (pl)	مواد تجميل
face mask	mask (m)	ماسك
manicure	monekīr (m)	مونيكير
to have a manicure	ʿamal monikīr	عمل مونيكير
pedicure	badikīr (m)	باديكير
make-up bag	ʃanṭet mekyāʒ (f)	شنطة مكياج
face powder	bodret weʃ (f)	بودرة وش
powder compact	ʿelbet bodra (f)	علبة بودرة
blusher	aḥmar χodūd (m)	أحمر خدود
perfume (bottled)	barfān (m)	بارفان
toilet water (lotion)	kolonya (f)	كولونيا
lotion	loʃion (m)	لوشن
cologne	kolonya (f)	كولونيا
eyeshadow	eyeʃadow (m)	ايّ شادو
eyeliner	koḥl (m)	كحل
mascara	maskara (f)	ماسكارا
lipstick	rūʒ (m)	روج
nail polish, enamel	monekīr (m)	مونيكير
hair spray	mosabbet el ʃaʿr (m)	مثبّت الشعر
deodorant	mozīl ʿaraʾ (m)	مزيل عرق
cream	krīm (m)	كريم
face cream	krīm lel weʃ (m)	كريم للوش
hand cream	krīm eyd (m)	كريم أيد
anti-wrinkle cream	krīm moḍād lel tagaʿīd (m)	كريم مضاد للتجاعيد
day cream	krīm en nahār (m)	كريم النهار
night cream	krīm el leyl (m)	كريم الليل
day (as adj)	nahāry	نهاري
night (as adj)	layly	ليّلي
tampon	tambon (m)	تانبون
toilet paper (toilet roll)	waraʾ twalet (m)	ورق تواليت
hair dryer	seʃwār (m)	سشوار

40. Watches. Clocks

watch (wristwatch)	sāʿa (f)	ساعة
dial	wag-h el sāʿa (m)	وجه الساعة
hand (of clock, watch)	ʿaʾrab el sāʿa (m)	عقرب الساعة
metal watch band	ʃerīʾṭ sāʿa maʿdaniya (m)	شريط ساعة معدنية
watch strap	ʃerīʾṭ el sāʿa (m)	شريط الساعة
battery	baṭṭariya (f)	بطّاريّة
to be dead (battery)	χelṣet	خلصت
to change a battery	ɣayar el baṭṭariya	غيّر البطّاريّة
to run fast	sabaʾ	سبق

to run slow	ta'akχar	تأخّر
wall clock	sā'et ḥeyṭa (f)	ساعة حيطة
hourglass	sā'a ramliya (f)	ساعة رمليّة
sundial	sā'a ʃamsiya (f)	ساعة شمسيّة
alarm clock	monabbeh (m)	منبّه
watchmaker	sa'āty (m)	ساعاتي
to repair (vt)	ṣallaḥ	صلّح

EVERYDAY EXPERIENCE

T&P Books Publishing

41. Money

money	folūs (pl)	فلوس
currency exchange	taḥwīl ʻomla (m)	تحويل عملة
exchange rate	seʻr el ṣarf (m)	سعر الصرف
ATM	makinet ṣarrāf ʼāly (f)	ماكينة صرّاف آلي
coin	ʼerʃ (m)	قرش
dollar	dolār (m)	دولار
euro	yoro (m)	يورو
lira	lira (f)	ليرة
Deutschmark	el mark el almāny (m)	المارك الألماني
franc	frank (m)	فرنك
pound sterling	geneyh esterlīny (m)	جنيه استرليني
yen	yen (m)	ين
debt	deyn (m)	دين
debtor	modīn (m)	مدين
to lend (money)	sallef	سلّف
to borrow (vi, vt)	estalaf	إستلف
bank	bank (m)	بنك
account	ḥesāb (m)	حساب
to deposit (vt)	awdaʻ	أودع
to deposit into the account	awdaʻ fel ḥesāb	أودّع في الحساب
to withdraw (vt)	saḥab men el ḥesāb	سحب من الحساب
credit card	kredit kard (f)	كريدت كارد
cash	kæʃ (m)	كاش
check	ʃīk (m)	شيك
to write a check	katab ʃīk	كتب شيك
checkbook	daftar ʃikāt (m)	دفتر شيكات
wallet	maḥfaẓa (f)	محفظة
change purse	maḥfazet fakka (f)	محفظة فكّة
safe	χazzāna (f)	خزّانة
heir	wāres (m)	وارث
inheritance	werāsa (f)	وراثة
fortune (wealth)	sarwa (f)	ثروّة
lease	ʻaʼd el egār (m)	عقد الإيجار
rent (money)	ogret el sakan (f)	أجرة السكن
to rent (sth from sb)	estʼgar	إستأجر
price	seʻr (m)	سعر

cost	taman (m)	ثمن
sum	mablaɣ (m)	مبلغ
to spend (vt)	ṣaraf	صرف
expenses	maṣarīf (pl)	مصاريف
to economize (vi, vt)	waffar	وفّر
economical	mowaffer	موّفر
to pay (vi, vt)	dafaʿ	دفع
payment	dafʿ (m)	دفع
change (give the ~)	el bā'y (m)	الباقي
tax	ḍarība (f)	ضريبة
fine	ɣarāma (f)	غرامة
to fine (vt)	faraḍ ɣarāma	فرض غرامة

42. Post. Postal service

post office	maktab el barīd (m)	مكتب البريد
mail (letters, etc.)	el barīd (m)	البريد
mailman	sāʿy el barīd (m)	ساعي البريد
opening hours	aw'āt el ʿamal (pl)	أوقات العمل
letter	resāla (f)	رسالة
registered letter	resāla mosaggala (f)	رسالة مسجّلة
postcard	kart barīdy (m)	كرت بريدي
telegram	barqiya (f)	برقيّة
package (parcel)	ṭard (m)	طرد
money transfer	ḥewāla māliya (f)	حوالة مالية
to receive (vt)	estalam	إستلم
to send (vt)	arsal	أرسل
sending	ersāl (m)	إرسال
address	ʿenwān (m)	عنوان
ZIP code	raqam el barīd (m)	رقم البريد
sender	morsel (m)	مرسل
receiver	morsel elayh (m)	مرسل إليه
name (first name)	esm (m)	اسم
surname (last name)	esm el ʿa'ela (m)	اسم العائلة
postage rate	taʿrīfa (f)	تعريفة
standard (adj)	ʿādy	عادي
economical (adj)	mowaffer	موّفر
weight	wazn (m)	وزن
to weigh (~ letters)	wazan	وزن
envelope	ẓarf (m)	ظرف
postage stamp	ṭābeʿ (m)	طابع
to stamp an envelope	alṣaq ṭābeʿ	ألصق طابع

43. Banking

bank	bank (m)	بنك
branch (of bank, etc.)	far' (m)	فرع
bank clerk, consultant	mowazzaf bank (m)	موظّف بنك
manager (director)	modīr (m)	مدير
bank account	ḥesāb bank (m)	حساب بنك
account number	raqam el ḥesāb (m)	رقم الحساب
checking account	ḥesāb gāry (m)	حساب جاري
savings account	ḥesāb tawfīr (m)	حساب توّفير
to open an account	fataḥ ḥesāb	فتح حساب
to close the account	'afal ḥesāb	قفل حساب
to deposit into the account	awda' fel ḥesāb	أودع في الحساب
to withdraw (vt)	saḥab men el ḥesāb	سحب من الحساب
deposit	wadee'a (f)	وديعة
to make a deposit	awda'	أودع
wire transfer	ḥewāla maṣrefiya (f)	حوالة مصرفيّة
to wire, to transfer	ḥawwel	حوّل
sum	mablaɣ (m)	مبلغ
How much?	kām?	كام؟
signature	tawqee' (m)	توقيع
to sign (vt)	waqqa'	وقّع
credit card	kredit kard (f)	كريدت كارد
code (PIN code)	kōd (m)	كود
credit card number	raqam el kredit kard (m)	رقم الكريدت كارد
ATM	makinet ṣarrāf 'āly (f)	ماكينة صرّاف آلي
check	ʃīk (m)	شيك
to write a check	katab ʃīk	كتب شيك
checkbook	daftar ʃikāt (m)	دفتر شيكات
loan (bank ~)	qarḍ (m)	قرض
to apply for a loan	'addem ṭalab 'ala qarḍ	قدّم طلب على قرض
to get a loan	ḥaṣal 'ala qarḍ	حصل على قرض
to give a loan	edda qarḍ	ادّى قرض
guarantee	ḍamān (m)	ضمان

44. Telephone. Phone conversation

telephone	telefon (m)	تليفون
cell phone	mobile (m)	موبايل
answering machine	gehāz radd 'alal mokalmāt (m)	جهاز ردّ على المكالمات

to call (by phone)	ettaṣal	إتّصل
phone call	mokalma telefoniya (f)	مكالمة تليفونية
to dial a number	ettaṣal be raqam	إتّصل برقم
Hello!	alo!	ألو!
to ask (vt)	sa'al	سأل
to answer (vi, vt)	radd	ردّ
to hear (vt)	seme'	سمع
well (adv)	kewayes	كويّس
not well (adv)	meʃ kowayīs	مش كويّس
noises (interference)	taʃwīʃ (m)	تشويش
receiver	sammā'a (f)	سمّاعة
to pick up (~ the phone)	rafa' el sammā'a	رفع السمّاعة
to hang up (~ the phone)	'afal el sammā'a	قفل السمّاعة
busy (engaged)	maʃɣūl	مشغول
to ring (ab. phone)	rann	رنّ
telephone book	dalīl el telefone (m)	دليل التليفون
local (adj)	maḥalliyya	ة محلّيّ
local call	mokalma maḥalliya (f)	مكالمة محلّيّة
long distance (~ call)	bi'īd	بعيد
long-distance call	mokalma bi'īda (f)	مكالمة بعيدة المدى
international (adj)	dowly	دوّلي
international call	mokalma dowliya (f)	مكالمة دوليّة

45. Cell phone

cell phone	mobile (m)	موبايل
display	'arḍ (m)	عرض
button	zerr (m)	زرّ
SIM card	sim kard (m)	سيم كارد
battery	baṭṭariya (f)	بطّاريّة
to be dead (battery)	χelṣet	خلصت
charger	ʃāḥen (m)	شاحن
menu	qā'ema (f)	قائمة
settings	awḍā' (pl)	أوضاع
tune (melody)	naɣama (f)	نغمة
to select (vt)	eχtār	إختار
calculator	'āla ḥasba (f)	آلة حاسبة
voice mail	barīd ṣawty (m)	بريد صوتي
alarm clock	monabbeh (m)	منبّه
contacts	gehāt el etteṣāl (pl)	جهات الإتّصال
SMS (text message)	resāla 'aṣīra ɛsɛmɛs (f)	رسالة قصيرة sms
subscriber	moʃtarek (m)	مشترك

46. Stationery

ballpoint pen	ʾalam gāf (m)	قلم جاف
fountain pen	ʾalam rīʃa (m)	قلم ريشة
pencil	ʾalam roṣāṣ (m)	قلم رصاص
highlighter	markar (m)	ماركر
felt-tip pen	ʾalam fulumaster (m)	قلم فلوماستر
notepad	mozakkera (f)	مذكّرة
agenda (diary)	gadwal el aʿmāl (m)	جدول الأعمال
ruler	masṭara (f)	مسطرة
calculator	ʾāla ḥasba (f)	آلة حاسبة
eraser	astīka (f)	استيكة
thumbtack	dabbūs (m)	دبّوس
paper clip	dabbūs waraʾ (m)	دبّوس ورق
glue	ṣamɣ (m)	صمغ
stapler	dabbāsa (f)	دبّاسة
hole punch	χarrāma (m)	خرّامة
pencil sharpener	barrāya (f)	برّاية

47. Foreign languages

language	loɣa (f)	لغة
foreign (adj)	agnaby	أجنبيّ
foreign language	loɣa agnabiya (f)	لغة أجنبية
to study (vt)	daras	درس
to learn (language, etc.)	taʿallam	تعلّم
to read (vi, vt)	ʾara	قرأ
to speak (vi, vt)	kallem	كلّم
to understand (vt)	fehem	فهم
to write (vt)	katab	كتب
fast (adv)	bosorʿa	بسرعة
slowly (adv)	bo boṭʾ	ببطء
fluently (adv)	beṭalāqa	بطلاقة
rules	qawāʿed (pl)	قواعد
grammar	el naḥw wel ṣarf (m)	النحو والصرف
vocabulary	mofradāt el loɣa (pl)	مفردات اللغة
phonetics	ṣawtīāt (pl)	صوتيات
textbook	ketāb taʿlīm (m)	كتاب تعليم
dictionary	qamūs (m)	قاموس
teach-yourself book	ketāb taʿlīm zāty (m)	كتاب تعليم ذاتي
phrasebook	ketāb lel ʿebarāt el ʃāʾeʿa (m)	كتاب للعبارت الشائعة

cassette, tape	kasett (m)	كاسيت
videotape	ʃerīʾṭ video (m)	شريط فيديو
CD, compact disc	sidī (m)	سي دي
DVD	dividī (m)	دي في دي
alphabet	abgadiya (f)	أبجدية
to spell (vt)	tahagga	تهجّى
pronunciation	noṭʾ (m)	نطق
accent	lahga (f)	لهجة
with an accent	be lahga	بـ لهجة
without an accent	men ɣeyr lahga	من غير لهجة
word	kelma (f)	كلمة
meaning	maʿna (m)	معنى
course (e.g., a French ~)	dawra (f)	دورة
to sign up	saggel esmo	سجّل إسمه
teacher	modarres (m)	مدرّس
translation (process)	targama (f)	ترجمة
translation (text, etc.)	targama (f)	ترجمة
translator	motargem (m)	مترجم
interpreter	motargem fawwry (m)	مترجم فوّري
polyglot	ʿalīm beʿeddet loɣāt (m)	عليم بعدّة لغات
memory	zākera (f)	ذاكرة

MEALS. RESTAURANT

T&P Books Publishing

48. Table setting

spoon	maʿlaʾa (f)	معلقة
knife	sekkīna (f)	سكّينة
fork	ʃawka (f)	شوكة
cup (e.g., coffee ~)	fengān (m)	فنجان
plate (dinner ~)	ṭabaʾ (m)	طبق
saucer	ṭabaʾ fengān (m)	طبق فنجان
napkin (on table)	mandīl waraʾ (m)	منديل ورق
toothpick	χallet senān (f)	خلة سنان

49. Restaurant

restaurant	maṭʿam (m)	مطعم
coffee house	ʾahwa (f), kaféih (m)	قهوة ,كافيه
pub, bar	bār (m)	بار
tearoom	ṣalone ʃāy (m)	صالون شاي
waiter	garsone (m)	جرسون
waitress	garsona (f)	جرسونة
bartender	bārman (m)	بارمان
menu	qāʾemet el ṭaʿām (f)	قائمة طعام
wine list	qāʾemet el χomūr (f)	قائمة خمور
to book a table	ḥagaz sofra	حجز سفرة
course, dish	wagba (f)	وجبة
to order (meal)	ṭalab	طلب
to make an order	ṭalab	طلب
aperitif	ʃarāb (m)	شراب
appetizer	moqabbelāt (pl)	مقبّلات
dessert	ḥalawīāt (pl)	حلويّات
check	ḥesāb (m)	حساب
to pay the check	dafaʿ el ḥesāb	دفع الحساب
to give change	edda el bāʾy	ادّي الباقي
tip	baʾʃīʃ (m)	بقشيش

50. Meals

food	akl (m)	أكل
to eat (vi, vt)	akal	أكل

breakfast	foṭūr (m)	فطور
to have breakfast	feṭer	فطر
lunch	ɣada' (m)	غداء
to have lunch	etɣadda	إتغدّى
dinner	'aʃā' (m)	عشاء
to have dinner	et'asʃa	إتعشّى
appetite	ʃahiya (f)	شهيّة
Enjoy your meal!	bel hana wel ʃefa!	بالهنا والشفا!
to open (~ a bottle)	fataḥ	فتح
to spill (liquid)	dala'	دلق
to spill out (vi)	dala'	دلق
to boil (vi)	ɣely	غلى
to boil (vt)	ɣely	غلى
boiled (~ water)	maɣly	مغلي
to chill, cool down (vt)	barrad	برّد
to chill (vi)	barrad	برّد
taste, flavor	ṭa'm (m)	طعم
aftertaste	ṭa'm ma ba'd el mazāq (m)	طعم ما بعد المذاق
to slim down (lose weight)	χass	خسّ
diet	reʒīm (m)	رجيم
vitamin	vitamīn (m)	فيتامين
calorie	so'ra ḥarāriya (f)	سعرة حراريّة
vegetarian (n)	nabāty (m)	نباتي
vegetarian (adj)	nabāty	نباتي
fats (nutrient)	dohūn (pl)	دهون
proteins	brotenāt (pl)	بروتينات
carbohydrates	naʃawīāt (pl)	نشويّات
slice (of lemon, ham)	ʃarīḥa (f)	شريحة
piece (of cake, pie)	'eṭ'a (f)	قطعة
crumb (of bread, cake, etc.)	fattāta (f)	فتاتة

51. Cooked dishes

course, dish	wagba (f)	وجبة
cuisine	maṭbaχ (m)	مطبخ
recipe	waṣfa (f)	وصفة
portion	naṣīb (m)	نصيب
salad	solṭa (f)	سلطة
soup	ʃorba (f)	شوربة
clear soup (broth)	mara'a (m)	مرقة
sandwich (bread)	sandawitʃ (m)	ساندويتش

fried eggs	beyḍ ma'ly (m)	بيض مقلي
hamburger (beefburger)	hamburger (m)	هامبورجر
beefsteak	steak laḥm (m)	ستيك لحم
side dish	ṭaba' gāneby (m)	طبق جانبي
spaghetti	spaɣetti (m)	سباجيتي
mashed potatoes	baṭāṭes mahrūsa (f)	بطاطس مهروسة
pizza	bītza (f)	بيتزا
porridge (oatmeal, etc.)	'aṣīda (f)	عصيدة
omelet	omlette (m)	اومليت
boiled (e.g., ~ beef)	maslū'	مسلوق
smoked (adj)	modakχen	مدخّن
fried (adj)	ma'ly	مقلي
dried (adj)	mogaffaf	مجفّف
frozen (adj)	mogammad	مجمّد
pickled (adj)	meχallel	مخلّل
sweet (sugary)	mesakkar	مسكّر
salty (adj)	māleḥ	مالح
cold (adj)	bāred	بارد
hot (adj)	soχn	سخن
bitter (adj)	morr	مرّ
tasty (adj)	ḥelw	حلو
to cook in boiling water	sala'	سلق
to cook (dinner)	ḥaḍḍar	حضّر
to fry (vt)	'ala	قلي
to heat up (food)	sakχan	سخّن
to salt (vt)	rasʃ malḥ	رشّ ملح
to pepper (vt)	rasʃ felfel	رشّ فلفل
to grate (vt)	baraʃ	برش
peel (n)	'eʃra (f)	قشرة
to peel (vt)	'asʃar	قشّر

52. Food

meat	laḥma (f)	لحمة
chicken	ferāχ (m)	فراخ
Rock Cornish hen (poussin)	farrūg (m)	فرّوج
duck	baṭṭa (f)	بطّة
goose	wezza (f)	وزّة
game	ṣeyd (m)	صيد
turkey	dīk rūmy (m)	ديك رومي
pork	laḥm el χanazīr (m)	لحم الخنزير
veal	laḥm el 'egl (m)	لحم العجل
lamb	laḥm ḍāny (m)	لحم ضاني

beef	laḥm baqary (m)	لحم بقري
rabbit	laḥm arāneb (m)	لحم أرانب
sausage (bologna, pepperoni, etc.)	sogo'' (m)	سجق
vienna sausage (frankfurter)	sogo'' (m)	سجق
bacon	bakon (m)	بيكون
ham	hām(m)	هام
gammon	faχd χanzīr (m)	فخذ خنزير
pâté	maʿgūn laḥm (m)	معجون لحم
liver	kebda (f)	كبدة
hamburger (ground beef)	hamburger (m)	هامبورجر
tongue	lesān (m)	لسان
egg	beyḍa (f)	بيضة
eggs	beyḍ (m)	بيض
egg white	bayāḍ el beyḍ (m)	بياض البيض
egg yolk	ṣafār el beyḍ (m)	صفار البيض
fish	samak (m)	سمك
seafood	sīfūd (pl)	سي فود
caviar	kaviar (m)	كافيار
crab	kaboria (m)	كابوريا
shrimp	gammbary (m)	جمّبري
oyster	maḥār (m)	محار
spiny lobster	estakoza (m)	استاكوزا
octopus	aχṭabūṭ (m)	أخطبوط
squid	kalmāry (m)	كالماري
sturgeon	samak el ḥafʃ (m)	سمك الحفش
salmon	salamon (m)	سلمون
halibut	samak el halbūt (m)	سمك الهلبوت
cod	samak el qadd (m)	سمك القد
mackerel	makerel (m)	ماكريل
tuna	tuna (f)	تونة
eel	ḥankalīs (m)	حنكليس
trout	salamon mera''aṭ (m)	سلمون مرقّط
sardine	sardīn (m)	سردين
pike	samak el karāky (m)	سمك الكراكي
herring	renga (f)	رنجة
bread	ʿeyʃ (m)	عيش
cheese	gebna (f)	جبنة
sugar	sokkar (m)	سكّر
salt	melḥ (m)	ملح
rice	rozz (m)	رزّ
pasta (macaroni)	makaruna (f)	مكرونة

noodles	nūdles (f)	نودلز
butter	zebda (f)	زبدة
vegetable oil	zeyt (m)	زيت
sunflower oil	zeyt ʿabbād el ʃams (m)	زيت عبّاد الشمس
margarine	margarīn (m)	مارجرين
olives	zaytūn (m)	زيتون
olive oil	zeyt el zaytūn (m)	زيت الزيتون
milk	laban (m)	لبن
condensed milk	ḥalīb mokassaf (m)	حليب مكثّف
yogurt	zabādy (m)	زبادي
sour cream	kreyma ḥamḍa (f)	كريمة حامضة
cream (of milk)	krīma (f)	كريمة
mayonnaise	mayonnɛ:z (m)	مايونيز
buttercream	krīmet zebda (f)	كريمة زبدة
cereal grains (wheat, etc.)	ḥobūb ʾamḥ (pl)	حبوب قمح
flour	deʾīʾ (m)	دقيق
canned food	moʿallabāt (pl)	معلّبات
cornflakes	korn fleks (m)	كورن فليكس
honey	ʿasal (m)	عسل
jam	mrabba (m)	مربّى
chewing gum	lebān (m)	لبان

53. Drinks

water	meyāh (f)	مياه
drinking water	mayet ʃorb (m)	ميّة شرب
mineral water	maya maʿdaniya (f)	ميّة معدنية
still (adj)	rakeda	راكدة
carbonated (adj)	kanz	كانز
sparkling (adj)	kanz	كانز
ice	talg (m)	ثلج
with ice	bel talg	بالتلج
non-alcoholic (adj)	men ɣeyr koḥūl	من غير كحول
soft drink	maʃrūb ɣāzy (m)	مشروب غازي
refreshing drink	ḥāga saʾʾa (f)	حاجة ساقعة
lemonade	limonāta (f)	ليموناتة
liquors	maʃrūbāt koḥūliya (pl)	مشروبات كحولية
wine	χamra (f)	خمرة
white wine	nebīz abyaḍ (m)	نبيذ أبيض
red wine	nebī aḥmar (m)	نبيذ أحمر
liqueur	liqure (m)	ليكيور
champagne	ʃambania (f)	شمبانيا

vermouth	vermote (m)	فيرموت
whiskey	wiski (m)	ويسكي
vodka	vodka (f)	فودكا
gin	ʒin (m)	جين
cognac	konyāk (m)	كونياك
rum	rum (m)	رم
coffee	'ahwa (f)	قهوة
black coffee	'ahwa sāda (f)	قهوة سادة
coffee with milk	'ahwa bel ḥalīb (f)	قهوة بالحليب
cappuccino	kaputʃino (m)	كابتشينو
instant coffee	neskafe (m)	نيسكافيه
milk	laban (m)	لبن
cocktail	koktayl (m)	كوكتيل
milkshake	milk ʃejk (m)	ميلك شيك
juice	ʿaṣīr (m)	عصير
tomato juice	ʿaṣīr ṭamāṭem (m)	عصير طماطم
orange juice	ʿaṣīr bortoqāl (m)	عصير برتقال
freshly squeezed juice	ʿaṣīr freʃ (m)	عصير فريش
beer	bīra (f)	بيرة
light beer	bīra χafīfa (f)	بيرة خفيفة
dark beer	bīra ɣam'a (f)	بيرة غامقة
tea	ʃāy (m)	شاي
black tea	ʃāy aḥmar (m)	شاي أحمر
green tea	ʃāy aχḍar (m)	شاي أخضر

54. Vegetables

vegetables	χoḍār (pl)	خضار
greens	χoḍrawāt waraqiya (pl)	خضروات ورقية
tomato	ṭamāṭem (f)	طماطم
cucumber	χeyār (m)	خيار
carrot	gazar (m)	جزر
potato	baṭāṭes (f)	بطاطس
onion	baṣal (m)	بصل
garlic	tūm (m)	ثوم
cabbage	koronb (m)	كرنب
cauliflower	'arnabīṭ (m)	قرنبيط
Brussels sprouts	koronb broksel (m)	كرنب بروكسل
broccoli	brokkoli (m)	بركولي
beetroot	bangar (m)	بنجر
eggplant	bātengān (m)	باذنجان
zucchini	kōsa (f)	كوسة

pumpkin	qarʿ ʿasaly (m)	قرع عسلي
turnip	left (m)	لفت
parsley	baʾdūnes (m)	بقدونس
dill	ʃabat (m)	شبت
lettuce	χass (m)	خس
celery	karfas (m)	كرفس
asparagus	helione (m)	هليون
spinach	sabāneχ (m)	سبانخ
pea	besella (f)	بسلّة
beans	fūl (m)	فول
corn (maize)	dora (f)	ذرة
kidney bean	faṣolya (f)	فاصوليا
bell pepper	felfel (m)	فلفل
radish	fegl (m)	فجل
artichoke	χarʃūf (m)	خرشوف

55. Fruits. Nuts

fruit	faχa (f)	فاكهة
apple	toffāḥa (f)	تفّاحة
pear	komettra (f)	كمّثرى
lemon	lymūn (m)	ليمون
orange	bortoqāl (m)	برتقال
strawberry (garden ~)	farawla (f)	فراولة
mandarin	yosfy (m)	يوسفي
plum	barʾūʾ (m)	برقوق
peach	χawχa (f)	خوخة
apricot	meʃmeʃ (f)	مشمش
raspberry	tūt el ʿalīʾ el aḥmar (m)	توت العليق الأحمر
pineapple	ananās (m)	أناناس
banana	moze (m)	موز
watermelon	baṭṭīχ (m)	بطّيخ
grape	ʿenab (m)	عنب
cherry	karaz (m)	كرز
melon	ʃammām (f)	شمّام
grapefruit	grabe frūt (m)	جريب فروت
avocado	avokado (f)	افوكاتو
papaya	babāya (m)	ببايا
mango	manga (m)	مانجة
pomegranate	rommān (m)	رمان
redcurrant	keʃmeʃ aḥmar (m)	كشمش أحمر
blackcurrant	keʃmeʃ aswad (m)	كشمش أسود
gooseberry	ʿenab el saʿlab (m)	عنب الثعلب

bilberry	‘enab al aḥrāg (m)	عنب الأحراج
blackberry	tūt aswad (m)	توت أسود
raisin	zebīb (m)	زبيب
fig	tīn (m)	تين
date	tamr (m)	تمر
peanut	fūl sudāny (m)	فول سوداني
almond	loze (m)	لوز
walnut	‘eyn gamal (f)	عين الجمل
hazelnut	bondo’ (m)	بندق
coconut	goze el hend (m)	جوز هند
pistachios	fosto’ (m)	فستق

56. Bread. Candy

bakers' confectionery (pastry)	ḥalawīāt (pl)	حلويّات
bread	‘eyʃ (m)	عيش
cookies	baskawīt (m)	بسكويت
chocolate (n)	ʃokolāta (f)	شكولاتة
chocolate (as adj)	bel ʃokolāṭa	بالشكولاتة
candy (wrapped)	bonbony (m)	بونبوني
cake (e.g., cupcake)	keyka (f)	كيكة
cake (e.g., birthday ~)	torta (f)	تورتة
pie (e.g., apple ~)	feṭīra (f)	فطيرة
filling (for cake, pie)	ḥaʃwa (f)	حشوة
jam (whole fruit jam)	mrabba (m)	مربّى
marmalade	marmalād (f)	مرملاد
waffles	waffles (pl)	وافلز
ice-cream	’ays krīm (m)	آيس كريم
pudding	būding (m)	بودنج

57. Spices

salt	melḥ (m)	ملح
salty (adj)	māleḥ	مالِح
to salt (vt)	rasʃ malḥ	رشّ ملح
black pepper	felfel aswad (m)	فلفل أسوّد
red pepper (milled ~)	felfel aḥmar (m)	فلفل أحمر
mustard	mosṭarda (m)	مسطردة
horseradish	fegl ḥār (m)	فجل حار
condiment	bahār (m)	بهار
spice	bahār (m)	بهار

sauce	ṣalṣa (f)	صلصة
vinegar	χall (m)	خلّ
anise	yansūn (m)	ينسون
basil	rīḥān (m)	ريحان
cloves	ʾoronfol (m)	قرنفل
ginger	zangabīl (m)	زنجبيل
coriander	kozbora (f)	كزبرة
cinnamon	ʾerfa (f)	قرفة
sesame	semsem (m)	سمسم
bay leaf	waraʾ el ɣār (m)	ورق الغار
paprika	babrika (f)	بابريكا
caraway	karawya (f)	كراوية
saffron	zaʿfarān (m)	زعفران

PERSONAL INFORMATION. FAMILY

T&P Books Publishing

58. Personal information. Forms

name (first name)	esm (m)	اسم
surname (last name)	esm el 'a'ela (m)	اسم العائلة
date of birth	tarīχ el melād (m)	تاريخ الميلاد
place of birth	makān el melād (m)	مكان الميلاد
nationality	gensiya (f)	جنسيّة
place of residence	maqarr el eqāma (m)	مقرّ الإقامة
country	balad (m)	بلد
profession (occupation)	mehna (f)	مهنة
gender, sex	ginss (m)	جنس
height	ṭūl (m)	طول
weight	wazn (m)	وزن

59. Family members. Relatives

mother	walda (f)	والدة
father	wāled (m)	والد
son	walad (m)	ولد
daughter	bent (f)	بنت
younger daughter	el bent el saɣīra (f)	البنت الصغيرة
younger son	el ebn el saɣīr (m)	الابن الصغير
eldest daughter	el bent el kebīra (f)	البنت الكبيرة
eldest son	el ebn el kabīr (m)	الابن الكبير
brother	aχ (m)	أخ
elder brother	el aχ el kibīr (m)	الأخ الكبير
younger brother	el aχ el ṣoɣeyyir (m)	الأخ الصغير
sister	oχt (f)	أخت
elder sister	el uχt el kibīra (f)	الأخت الكبيرة
younger sister	el uχt el ṣoɣeyyira (f)	الأخت الصغيرة
cousin (masc.)	ibn 'amm (m), ibn χāl (m)	إبن عمّ, إبن خال
cousin (fem.)	bint 'amm (f), bint χāl (f)	بنت عم, بنت خال
mom, mommy	mama (f)	ماما
dad, daddy	baba (m)	بابا
parents	waldeyn (du)	والدين
child	ṭefl (m)	طفل
children	aṭfāl (pl)	أطفال
grandmother	gedda (f)	جدّة
grandfather	gadd (m)	جدّ

grandson	ḥafīd (m)	حفيد
granddaughter	ḥafīda (f)	حفيدة
grandchildren	aḥfād (pl)	أحفاد
uncle	ʿamm (m), χāl (m)	عمّ, خال
aunt	ʿamma (f), χāla (f)	عمة, خالة
nephew	ibn el aχ (m), ibn el uχt (m)	إبن الأخ, إبن الأخت
niece	bint el aχ (f), bint el uχt (f)	بنت الأخ, بنت الأخت
mother-in-law (wife's mother)	ḥamah (f)	حماة
father-in-law (husband's father)	ḥama (m)	حما
son-in-law (daughter's husband)	goze el bent (m)	جوز البنت
stepmother	merāt el abb (f)	مرات الأب
stepfather	goze el omm (m)	جوز الأم
infant	ṭefl raḍeeʿ (m)	طفل رضيع
baby (infant)	mawlūd (m)	موّلود
little boy, kid	walad ṣaɣīr (m)	ولد صغير
wife	goza (f)	جوزة
husband	goze (m)	جوز
spouse (husband)	goze (m)	جوز
spouse (wife)	goza (f)	جوزة
married (masc.)	metgawwez	متجوّز
married (fem.)	metgawweza	متجوّزة
single (unmarried)	aʿzab	أعزب
bachelor	aʿzab (m)	أعزب
divorced (masc.)	moṭallaq (m)	مطلّق
widow	armala (f)	أرملة
widower	armal (m)	أرمل
relative	ʾarīb (m)	قريب
close relative	nesīb ʾarīb (m)	نسيب قريب
distant relative	nesīb beʿīd (m)	نسيب بعيد
relatives	aqāreb (pl)	أقارب
orphan (boy or girl)	yatīm (m)	يتيم
guardian (of a minor)	walyī amr (m)	وليّ أمر
to adopt (a boy)	tabanna	تبنّى
to adopt (a girl)	tabanna	تبنّى

60. Friends. Coworkers

friend (masc.)	ṣadīq (m)	صديق
friend (fem.)	ṣadīqa (f)	صديقة
friendship	ṣadāqa (f)	صداقة
to be friends	ṣādaq	صادق

buddy (masc.)	ṣāḥeb (m)	صاحب
buddy (fem.)	ṣaḥba (f)	صاحبة
partner	rafī' (m)	رفيق
chief (boss)	ra'īs (m)	رئيس
superior (n)	el arfa' maqāman (m)	الأرفع مقاماً
owner, proprietor	ṣāḥib (m)	صاحب
subordinate (n)	tābe' (m)	تابع
colleague	zamīl (m)	زميل
acquaintance (person)	ma'refa (m)	معرفة
fellow traveler	rafī' safar (m)	رفيق سفر
classmate	zamīl fel ṣaff (m)	زميل في الصفّ
neighbor (masc.)	gār (m)	جار
neighbor (fem.)	gāra (f)	جارة
neighbors	gerān (pl)	جيران

HUMAN BODY. MEDICINE

T&P Books Publishing

61. Head

head	ra's (m)	رأس
face	weʃ (m)	وش
nose	manaχīr (m)	مناخير
mouth	bo' (m)	بوء
eye	ʿeyn (f)	عين
eyes	ʿoyūn (pl)	عيون
pupil	ḥad'a (f)	حدقة
eyebrow	ḥāgeb (m)	حاجب
eyelash	remʃ (m)	رمش
eyelid	gefn (m)	جفن
tongue	lesān (m)	لسان
tooth	senna (f)	سنّة
lips	ʃafāyef (pl)	شفايف
cheekbones	ʿaḍmet el χadd (f)	عضمة الخدّ
gum	lassa (f)	لثّة
palate	ḥanak (m)	حنك
nostrils	manaχer (pl)	مناخر
chin	da''n (m)	دقن
jaw	fakk (m)	فكّ
cheek	χadd (m)	خدّ
forehead	gabha (f)	جبهة
temple	ṣedɣ (m)	صدغ
ear	wedn (f)	ودن
back of the head	'afa (m)	قفا
neck	ra'aba (f)	رقبة
throat	zore (m)	زور
hair	ʃaʿr (m)	شعر
hairstyle	tasrīḥa (f)	تسريحة
haircut	tasrīḥa (f)	تسريحة
wig	barūka (f)	باروكة
mustache	ʃanab (pl)	شنب
beard	leḥya (f)	لحية
to have (a beard, etc.)	ʿando	عنده
braid	ḍefīra (f)	ضفيرة
sideburns	sawālef (pl)	سوالف
red-haired (adj)	aḥmar el ʃaʿr	أحمر الشعر
gray (hair)	ʃaʿr abyaḍ	شعر أبيض

bald (adj)	aṣlaʿ	أصلع
bald patch	ṣalaʿ (m)	صلع
ponytail	deyl ḥoṣān (m)	ديل حصان
bangs	ʾoṣṣa (f)	قصّة

62. Human body

hand	yad (m)	يد
arm	derāʿ (f)	دراع
finger	ṣobāʿ (m)	صباع
toe	ṣobāʿ el ʾadam (m)	صباع القدم
thumb	ebhām (m)	إبهام
little finger	χonṣor (m)	خنصر
nail	ḍefr (m)	ضفر
fist	qabḍa (f)	قبضة
palm	kaff (f)	كفّ
wrist	meʿṣam (m)	معصم
forearm	sāʿed (m)	ساعد
elbow	kūʿ (m)	كوع
shoulder	ketf (f)	كتف
leg	regl (f)	رجل
foot	qadam (f)	قدم
knee	rokba (f)	ركبة
calf (part of leg)	semmāna (f)	سمّانة
hip	faχd (f)	فخد
heel	kaʿb (m)	كعب
body	gesm (m)	جسم
stomach	baṭn (m)	بطن
chest	ṣedr (m)	صدر
breast	sady (m)	ثدي
flank	ganb (m)	جنب
back	ḍahr (m)	ضهر
lower back	asfal el ḍahr (m)	أسفل الضهر
waist	wesṭ (f)	وسط
navel (belly button)	sorra (f)	سرّة
buttocks	ardāf (pl)	أرداف
bottom	debr (m)	دبر
beauty mark	ʃāma (f)	شامة
birthmark (café au lait spot)	waḥma	وحمة
tattoo	waʃm (m)	وشم
scar	nadba (f)	ندبة

63. Diseases

sickness	maraḍ (m)	مرض
to be sick	mereḍ	مرض
health	ṣeḥḥa (f)	صحّة
runny nose (coryza)	raʃ-ḥ fel anf (m)	رشح في الأنف
tonsillitis	eltehāb el lawzateyn (m)	إلتهاب اللوزتين
cold (illness)	zokām (m)	زكام
to catch a cold	gālo bard	جاله برد
bronchitis	eltehāb ʃoʻaby (m)	إلتهاب شعبيّ
pneumonia	eltehāb raʾawy (m)	إلتهاب رئوي
flu, influenza	influenza (f)	إنفلونزا
nearsighted (adj)	ʾaṣīr el naẓar	قصير النظر
farsighted (adj)	beʻīd el naẓar	بعيد النظر
strabismus (crossed eyes)	ḥawal (m)	حوّل
cross-eyed (adj)	aḥwal	أحوّل
cataract	katarakt (f)	كاتاراكت
glaucoma	glawkoma (f)	جلوكوما
stroke	sakta (f)	سكتة
heart attack	azma ʾalbiya (f)	أزمة قلبية
myocardial infarction	nawba ʾalbiya (f)	نوبة قلبية
paralysis	ʃalal (m)	شلل
to paralyze (vt)	ʃall	شلّ
allergy	ḥasasiya (f)	حساسيّة
asthma	rabw (m)	ربو
diabetes	dāʾ el sokkary (m)	داء السكّري
toothache	alam asnān (m)	ألم الأسنان
caries	naχr el asnān (m)	نخر الأسنان
diarrhea	es-hāl (m)	إسهال
constipation	emsāk (m)	إمساك
stomach upset	eḍṭrāb el meʻda (m)	إضطراب المعدة
food poisoning	tasammom (m)	تسمم
to get food poisoning	etsammem	إتسمّم
arthritis	eltehāb el mafāṣel (m)	إلتهاب المفاصل
rickets	kosāḥ el aṭfāl (m)	كساح الأطفال
rheumatism	rheumatism (m)	روماتزم
atherosclerosis	taṣṣallob el ʃarayīn (m)	تصلّب الشرايين
gastritis	eltehāb el meʻda (m)	إلتهاب المعدة
appendicitis	eltehāb el zayda el dūdiya (m)	إلتهاب الزائدة الدودية
cholecystitis	eltehāb el marāra (m)	إلتهاب المرارة
ulcer	qorḥa (f)	قرحة

measles	maraḍ el ḥaṣba (m)	مرض الحصبة
rubella (German measles)	el ḥaṣba el almaniya (f)	الحصبة الألمانية
jaundice	yaraqān (m)	يرقان
hepatitis	eltehāb el kabed el vayrūsy (m)	إلتهاب الكبد الفيروسي
schizophrenia	fuṣām (m)	فصام
rabies (hydrophobia)	dā' el kalb (m)	داء الكلب
neurosis	edṭrāb 'aṣaby (m)	إضطراب عصبي
concussion	ertegāg el moχ (m)	إرتجاج المخ
cancer	saraṭān (m)	سرطان
sclerosis	taṣṣallob (m)	تصلّب
multiple sclerosis	taṣṣallob mota'added (m)	تصلّب متعدّد
alcoholism	edmān el χamr (m)	إدمان الخمر
alcoholic (n)	modmen el χamr (m)	مدمن الخمر
syphilis	syfilis el zehry (m)	سفلس الزهري
AIDS	el eydz (m)	الايدز
tumor	waram (m)	ورم
malignant (adj)	χabīs	خبيث
benign (adj)	ḥamīd (m)	حميد
fever	ḥomma (f)	حمّى
malaria	malaria (f)	ملاريا
gangrene	ɣanɣarīna (f)	غنغرينا
seasickness	dawār el baḥr (m)	دوار البحر
epilepsy	maraḍ el ṣara' (m)	مرض الصرع
epidemic	wabā' (m)	وباء
typhus	tyfus (m)	تيفوس
tuberculosis	maraḍ el soll (m)	مرض السلّ
cholera	kōlīra (f)	كوليرا
plague (bubonic ~)	ṭa'ūn (m)	طاعون

64. Symptoms. Treatments. Part 1

symptom	'araḍ (m)	عرض
temperature	ḥarāra (f)	حرارة
high temperature (fever)	ḥomma (f)	حمّى
pulse	nabḍ (m)	نبض
dizziness (vertigo)	dawχa (f)	دوخة
hot (adj)	soχn	سخن
shivering	ra'ʃa (f)	رعشة
pale (e.g., ~ face)	aṣfar	أصفر
cough	koḥḥa (f)	كحّة
to cough (vi)	kaḥḥ	كحّ

to sneeze (vi)	ʿaṭas	عطس
faint	dawχa (f)	دوخة
to faint (vi)	oɣma ʿaleyh	أغمي عليه
bruise (hématome)	kadma (f)	كدمة
bump (lump)	tawarrom (m)	تورّم
to bang (bump)	etχabaṭ	إتخبط
contusion (bruise)	raḍḍa (f)	رضّة
to get a bruise	etkadam	إتكدم
to limp (vi)	ʿarag	عرج
dislocation	χalʿ (m)	خلع
to dislocate (vt)	χalaʿ	خلع
fracture	kasr (m)	كسر
to have a fracture	enkasar	إنكسر
cut (e.g., paper ~)	garḥ (m)	جرح
to cut oneself	garaḥ nafsoh	جرح نفسه
bleeding	nazīf (m)	نزيف
burn (injury)	ḥarʾ (m)	حرق
to get burned	et-ḥaraʾ	إتحرق
to prick (vt)	waχaz	وخز
to prick oneself	waχaz nafso	وخز نفسه
to injure (vt)	aṣāb	أصاب
injury	eṣāba (f)	إصابة
wound	garḥ (m)	جرح
trauma	ṣadma (f)	صدمة
to be delirious	haza	هذى
to stutter (vi)	talaʿsam	تلعثم
sunstroke	ḍarabet ʃams (f)	ضربة شمس

65. Symptoms. Treatments. Part 2

pain, ache	alam (m)	ألم
splinter (in foot, etc.)	ʃazya (f)	شظية
sweat (perspiration)	ʿerʾ (m)	عرق
to sweat (perspire)	ʿereʾ	عرق
vomiting	targeeʿ (m)	ترجيع
convulsions	taʃonnogāt (pl)	تشنّجات
pregnant (adj)	ḥāmel	حامل
to be born	etwalad	اتولّد
delivery, labor	welāda (f)	ولادة
to deliver (~ a baby)	walad	ولد
abortion	eg-hāḍ (m)	إجهاض
breathing, respiration	tanaffos (m)	تنفّس

in-breath (inhalation)	estenʃāq (m)	إستنشاق
out-breath (exhalation)	zafīr (m)	زفير
to exhale (breathe out)	zafar	زفر
to inhale (vi)	estanʃaq	إستنشق
disabled person	mo'āq (m)	معاق
cripple	moq'ad (m)	مقعد
drug addict	modmen moχaddarāt (m)	مدمن مخدّرات
deaf (adj)	aṭraʃ	أطرش
mute (adj)	aχras	أخرس
deaf mute (adj)	aṭraʃ aχras	أطرش أخرس
mad, insane (adj)	magnūn (m)	مجنون
madman (demented person)	magnūn (m)	مجنون
madwoman	magnūna (f)	مجنونة
to go insane	etgannen	اتجنّن
gene	ʒīn (m)	جين
immunity	manā'a (f)	مناعة
hereditary (adj)	werāsy	وراثي
congenital (adj)	χolqy men el welāda	خلقي من الولادة
virus	virūs (m)	فيروس
microbe	mikrūb (m)	ميكروب
bacterium	garsūma (f)	جرثومة
infection	'adwa (f)	عدوى

66. Symptoms. Treatments. Part 3

hospital	mostaʃfa (m)	مستشفى
patient	marīḍ (m)	مريض
diagnosis	taʃχīṣ (m)	تشخيص
cure	ʃefā' (m)	شفاء
medical treatment	'elāg ṭebby (m)	علاج طبي
to get treatment	et'āleg	اتعالج
to treat (~ a patient)	'ālag	عالج
to nurse (look after)	marraḍ	مرّض
care (nursing ~)	'enāya (f)	عناية
operation, surgery	'amaliya grāḥiya (f)	عمليّة جراحية
to bandage (head, limb)	ḍammad	ضمّد
bandaging	taḍmīd (m)	تضميد
vaccination	talqīḥ (m)	تلقيح
to vaccinate (vt)	laqqaḥ	لقّح
injection, shot	ḥo'na (f)	حقنة
to give an injection	ḥa'an ebra	حقن إبرة

attack	nawba (f)	نوبة
amputation	batr (m)	بتر
to amputate (vt)	batr	بتر
coma	ɣaybūba (f)	غيبوبة
to be in a coma	kān fi ḥālet ɣaybūba	كان في حالة غيبوبة
intensive care	el ʿenāya el morakkaza (f)	العناية المركّزة
to recover (~ from flu)	ʃefy	شفي
condition (patient's ~)	ḥāla (f)	حالة
consciousness	waʿy (m)	وعي
memory (faculty)	zākera (f)	ذاكرة
to pull out (tooth)	χalaʿ	خلع
filling	ḥaʃww (m)	حشوّ
to fill (a tooth)	ḥaʃa	حشا
hypnosis	el tanwīm el meɣnaṭīsy (m)	التنويم المغناطيسى
to hypnotize (vt)	nawwem	نوّم

67. Medicine. Drugs. Accessories

medicine, drug	dawāʾ (m)	دواء
remedy	ʿelāg (m)	علاج
to prescribe (vt)	waṣaf	وصف
prescription	waṣfa (f)	وصفة
tablet, pill	ʾorṣ (m)	قرص
ointment	marham (m)	مرهم
ampule	ambūla (f)	أمبولة
mixture	dawāʾ ʃorb (m)	دواء شراب
syrup	ʃarāb (m)	شراب
pill	ḥabba (f)	حبّة
powder	zorūr (m)	ذرور
gauze bandage	ḍammāda ʃāʃ (f)	ضمادة شاش
cotton wool	ʾoṭn (m)	قطن
iodine	yūd (m)	يود
Band-Aid	blaster (m)	بلاستر
eyedropper	ʾaṭṭāra (f)	قطّارة
thermometer	termometr (m)	ترمومتر
syringe	serennga (f)	سرنّجة
wheelchair	korsy motaḥarrek (m)	كرسي متحرك
crutches	ʿokkāz (m)	عكّاز
painkiller	mosakken (m)	مسكّن
laxative	molayen (m)	مليّن
spirits (ethanol)	etanol (m)	إيثانول
medicinal herbs	aʿʃāb ṭebbiya (pl)	أعشاب طبّية
herbal (~ tea)	ʿoʃby	عشبي

APARTMENT

T&P Books Publishing

68. Apartment

apartment	ʃa''a (f)	شقّة
room	oḍa (f)	أوضة
bedroom	oḍet el nome (f)	أوضة النوم
dining room	oḍet el sofra (f)	أوضة السفرة
living room	oḍet el esteqbāl (f)	أوضة الإستقبال
study (home office)	maktab (m)	مكتب
entry room	madχal (m)	مدخل
bathroom (room with a bath or shower)	ḥammām (m)	حمّام
half bath	ḥammām (m)	حمّام
ceiling	sa'f (m)	سقف
floor	arḍiya (f)	أرضية
corner	zawya (f)	زاوية

69. Furniture. Interior

furniture	asās (m)	أثاث
table	maktab (m)	مكتب
chair	korsy (m)	كرسي
bed	serīr (m)	سرير
couch, sofa	kanaba (f)	كنبة
armchair	korsy (m)	كرسي
bookcase	χazzānet kotob (f)	خزّانة كتب
shelf	raff (m)	رفّ
wardrobe	dolāb (m)	دولاب
coat rack (wall-mounted ~)	ʃammā'a (f)	شمّاعة
coat stand	ʃammā'a (f)	شمّاعة
bureau, dresser	dolāb adrāg (m)	دولاب أدراج
coffee table	ṭarabeyzet el 'ahwa (f)	طرابيزة القهوة
mirror	merāya (f)	مراية
carpet	seggāda (f)	سجّادة
rug, small carpet	seggāda (f)	سجّادة
fireplace	daffāya (f)	دفّاية
candle	ʃam'a (f)	شمعة
candlestick	ʃam'adān (m)	شمعدان

drapes	satā'er (pl)	ستائر
wallpaper	wara' ḥā'eṭ (m)	ورق حائط
blinds (jalousie)	satā'er ofoqiya (pl)	ستائر أفقيّة
table lamp	abāʒūr (f)	اباجورة
wall lamp (sconce)	lammbet ḥā'eṭ (f)	لمّبة حائط
floor lamp	meṣbāḥ arḍy (m)	مصباح أرضي
chandelier	nagafa (f)	نجفة
leg (of chair, table)	regl (f)	رجل
armrest	masnad (m)	مسند
back (backrest)	masnad (m)	مسند
drawer	dorg (m)	درج

70. Bedding

bedclothes	bayāḍāt el serīr (pl)	بياضات السرير
pillow	maχadda (f)	مخدّة
pillowcase	kīs el maχadda (m)	كيس المخدّة
duvet, comforter	leḥāf (m)	لحاف
sheet	melāya (f)	ملاية
bedspread	ɣaṭā' el serīr (m)	غطاء السرير

71. Kitchen

kitchen	maṭbaχ (m)	مطبخ
gas	ɣāz (m)	غاز
gas stove (range)	botoɣāz (m)	بوتوغاز
electric stove	forn kaharabā'y (m)	فرن كهربائي
oven	forn (m)	فرن
microwave oven	mikroweyv (m)	ميكروويف
refrigerator	tallāga (f)	ثلاجة
freezer	freyzer (m)	فريزر
dishwasher	ɣassālet aṭbā' (f)	غسّالة أطباق
meat grinder	farrāmet laḥm (f)	فرّامة لحم
juicer	'aṣṣāra (f)	عصّارة
toaster	maḥmaṣet χobz (f)	محمصة خبز
mixer	χallāṭ (m)	خلّاط
coffee machine	makinet ṣon' el 'ahwa (f)	ماكينة صنع القهوة
coffee pot	ɣallāya kahraba'iya (f)	غلّاية القهوة
coffee grinder	maṭ-ḥanet 'ahwa (f)	مطحنة قهوة
kettle	ɣallāya (f)	غلّاية
teapot	barrād el ʃāy (m)	برّاد الشاي
lid	ɣaṭā' (m)	غطاء

tea strainer	maṣfāh el ʃāy (f)	مصفاة الشاي
spoon	maʿlaʾa (f)	معلقة
teaspoon	maʿlaʾet ʃāy (f)	معلقة شاي
soup spoon	maʿlaʾa kebīra (f)	ملعقة كبيرة
fork	ʃawka (f)	شوكة
knife	sekkīna (f)	سكّينة
tableware (dishes)	awāny (pl)	أواني
plate (dinner ~)	ṭabaʾ (m)	طبق
saucer	ṭabaʾ fengān (m)	طبق فنجان
shot glass	kāsa (f)	كاسة
glass (tumbler)	kobbāya (f)	كوبّاية
cup	fengān (m)	فنجان
sugar bowl	sokkariya (f)	سكّريّة
salt shaker	mamlaḥa (f)	مملحة
pepper shaker	mobhera (f)	مبهرة
butter dish	ṭabaʾ zebda (m)	طبق زبدة
stock pot (soup pot)	ḥalla (f)	حلّة
frying pan (skillet)	ṭāsa (f)	طاسة
ladle	maɣrafa (f)	مغرفة
colander	maṣfāh (f)	مصفاه
tray (serving ~)	ṣeniya (f)	صينيّة
bottle	ezāza (f)	إزازة
jar (glass)	barṭamān (m)	برطمان
can	kanz (m)	كانز
bottle opener	fattāḥa (f)	فتّاحة
can opener	fattāḥa (f)	فتّاحة
corkscrew	barrīma (f)	بريمة
filter	filter (m)	فلتر
to filter (vt)	ṣaffa	صفّى
trash, garbage (food waste, etc.)	zebāla (f)	زبالة
trash can (kitchen ~)	ṣandūʾ el zebāla (m)	صندوق الزبالة

72. Bathroom

bathroom	ḥammām (m)	حمّام
water	meyāh (f)	مياه
faucet	ḥanafiya (f)	حنفيّة
hot water	maya soχna (f)	مايّة سخنة
cold water	maya barda (f)	مايّة باردة
toothpaste	maʿgūn asnān (m)	معجون أسنان
to brush one's teeth	naḍḍaf el asnān	نظّف الأسنان

toothbrush	forʃet senān (f)	فرشة أسنان
to shave (vi)	ḥala'	حلق
shaving foam	raɣwa lel ḥelā'a (f)	رغوة للحلاقة
razor	mūs (m)	موس
to wash (one's hands, etc.)	ɣasal	غسل
to take a bath	estaḥamma	إستحمّى
shower	doʃ (m)	دوش
to take a shower	aχad doʃ	أخد دوش
bathtub	banyo (m)	بانيو
toilet (toilet bowl)	twalet (m)	تواليت
sink (washbasin)	ḥoḍe (m)	حوض
soap	ṣabūn (m)	صابون
soap dish	ṣabbāna (f)	صبّانة
sponge	līfa (f)	ليفة
shampoo	ʃambū (m)	شامبو
towel	fūṭa (f)	فوطة
bathrobe	robe el ḥammām (m)	روب حمّام
laundry (process)	ɣasīl (m)	غسيل
washing machine	ɣassāla (f)	غسّالة
to do the laundry	ɣasal el malābes	غسل الملابس
laundry detergent	mas-ḥū' ɣasīl (m)	مسحوق غسيل

73. Household appliances

TV set	televizion (m)	تليفزيون
tape recorder	gehāz tasgīl (m)	جهاز تسجيل
VCR (video recorder)	'āla tasgīl video (f)	آلة تسجيل فيديو
radio	gehāz radio (m)	جهاز راديو
player (CD, MP3, etc.)	blayer (m)	بليير
video projector	gehāz 'arḍ (m)	جهاز عرض
home movie theater	sinema manzeliya (f)	سينما منزليّة
DVD player	dividī blayer (m)	دي في دي بليير
amplifier	mokabbaer el ṣote (m)	مكبّر الصوت
video game console	'ātāry (m)	أتاري
video camera	kamera video (f)	كاميرا فيديو
camera (photo)	kamera (f)	كاميرا
digital camera	kamera diʒital (f)	كاميرا ديجيتال
vacuum cleaner	maknasa kahraba'iya (f)	مكنسة كهربائيّة
iron (e.g., steam ~)	makwa (f)	مكواة
ironing board	lawḥet kayī (f)	لوحة كيّ
telephone	telefon (m)	تليفون
cell phone	mobile (m)	موبايل

typewriter	ʾāla katba (f)	آلة كاتبة
sewing machine	makanet el χeyāṭa (f)	مكنة الخياطة
microphone	mikrofon (m)	ميكروفون
headphones	sammaʿāt raʾsiya (pl)	سمّاعات رأسية
remote control (TV)	remowt kontrol (m)	ريموت كنترول
CD, compact disc	sidī (m)	سي دي
cassette, tape	kasett (m)	كاسيت
vinyl record	esṭewāna mūsīqa (f)	أسطوانة موسيقى

THE EARTH. WEATHER

T&P Books Publishing

74. Outer space

space	faḍā' (m)	فضاء
space (as adj)	faḍā'y	فضائي
outer space	el faḍā' el χāregy (m)	الفضاء الخارجي
world	'ālam (m)	عالم
universe	el kōn (m)	الكون
galaxy	el magarra (f)	المجرّة
star	negm (m)	نجم
constellation	borg (m)	برج
planet	kawwkab (m)	كوكب
satellite	'amar ṣenā'y (m)	قمر صناعي
meteorite	nayzek (m)	نيّزك
comet	mozannab (m)	مذنّب
asteroid	kowaykeb (m)	كويكب
orbit	madār (m)	مدار
to revolve (~ around the Earth)	dār	دار
atmosphere	el ɣelāf el gawwy (m)	الغلاف الجوّي
the Sun	el ʃams (f)	الشمس
solar system	el magmū'a el ʃamsiya (f)	المجموعة الشمسيّة
solar eclipse	kosūf el ʃams (m)	كسوف الشمس
the Earth	el arḍ (f)	الأرض
the Moon	el 'amar (m)	القمر
Mars	el marrīχ (m)	المرّيخ
Venus	el zahra (f)	الزهرة
Jupiter	el moʃtary (m)	المشتري
Saturn	zoḥḥol (m)	زحل
Mercury	'aṭāred (m)	عطارد
Uranus	uranus (m)	اورانوس
Neptune	nibtūn (m)	نبتون
Pluto	bluto (m)	بلوتو
Milky Way	darb el tebbāna (m)	درب التبّانة
Great Bear (Ursa Major)	el dobb el akbar (m)	الدب الأكبر
North Star	negm el 'oṭb (m)	نجم القطب
Martian	sāken el marrīχ (m)	ساكن المرّيخ
extraterrestrial (n)	faḍā'y (m)	فضائي

alien	kā'en fadā'y (m)	كائن فضائي
flying saucer	ṭaba' ṭā'er (m)	طبق طائر
spaceship	markaba faḍa'iya (f)	مركبة فضائية
space station	maḥaṭṭet faḍā' (f)	محطّة فضاء
blast-off	enṭelāq (m)	إنطلاق
engine	motore (m)	موتور
nozzle	manfaθ (m)	منفث
fuel	woqūd (m)	وقود
cockpit, flight deck	kabīna (f)	كابينة
antenna	hawā'y (m)	هوائي
porthole	kowwa mostadīra (f)	كوّة مستديرة
solar panel	lawḥa ʃamsiya (f)	لوحة شمسيّة
spacesuit	badlet el faḍā' (f)	بدّلة الفضاء
weightlessness	en'edām wazn (m)	إنعدام الوزن
oxygen	oksiʒīn (m)	أوكسجين
docking (in space)	rasw (m)	رسو
to dock (vi, vt)	rasa	رسى
observatory	marṣad (m)	مرصد
telescope	teleskop (m)	تلسكوب
to observe (vt)	rāqab	راقب
to explore (vt)	estakʃef	إستكشف

75. The Earth

the Earth	el arḍ (f)	الأرض
the globe (the Earth)	el kora el arḍiya (f)	الكرة الأرضيّة
planet	kawwkab (m)	كوّكب
atmosphere	el ɣelāf el gawwy (m)	الغلاف الجوّي
geography	goɣrafia (f)	جغرافيا
nature	ṭabee'a (f)	طبيعة
globe (table ~)	namūzag lel kora el arḍiya (m)	نموذج للكرة الأرضيّة
map	χarīṭa (f)	خريطة
atlas	aṭlas (m)	أطلس
Europe	orobba (f)	أوروبّا
Asia	asya (f)	آسيا
Africa	afreqia (f)	أفريقيا
Australia	ostorālya (f)	أستراليا
America	amrīka (f)	أمريكا
North America	amrīka el ʃamaliya (f)	أمريكا الشماليّة

South America	amrīka el ganūbiya (f)	أمريكا الجنوبيّة
Antarctica	el qoṭb el ganūby (m)	القطب الجنوبي
the Arctic	el qoṭb el ʃamāly (m)	القطب الشمالي

76. Cardinal directions

north	ʃemāl (m)	شمال
to the north	lel ʃamāl	للشمال
in the north	fel ʃamāl	في الشمال
northern (adj)	ʃamāly	شمالي
south	ganūb (m)	جنوب
to the south	lel ganūb	للجنوب
in the south	fel ganūb	في الجنوب
southern (adj)	ganūby	جنوبي
west	ɣarb (m)	غرب
to the west	lel ɣarb	للغرب
in the west	fel ɣarb	في الغرب
western (adj)	ɣarby	غربي
east	ʃarʾ (m)	شرق
to the east	lel ʃarʾ	للشرق
in the east	fel ʃarʾ	في الشرق
eastern (adj)	ʃarʾy	شرقي

77. Sea. Ocean

sea	baḥr (m)	بحر
ocean	moḥīṭ (m)	محيط
gulf (bay)	χalīg (m)	خليج
straits	maḍīq (m)	مضيق
land (solid ground)	barr (m)	برّ
continent (mainland)	qārra (f)	قارّة
island	gezīra (f)	جزيرة
peninsula	ʃebh gezeyra (f)	شبه جزيرة
archipelago	magmūʿet gozor (f)	مجموعة جزر
bay, cove	χalīg (m)	خليج
harbor	mināʾ (m)	ميناء
lagoon	lagūn (m)	لاجون
cape	raʾs (m)	رأس
atoll	gezīra morganiya estwaʾiya (f)	جزيزة مرجانيةّ إستوائيّة
reef	ʃoʿāb (pl)	شعاب
coral	morgān (m)	مرجان

coral reef	ʃoʿāb morganiya (pl)	شعاب مرجانية
deep (adj)	ʿamīq	عميق
depth (deep water)	ʿomq (m)	عمق
abyss	el ʿomq el saḥīq (m)	العمق السحيق
trench (e.g., Mariana ~)	χondoq (m)	خندق
current (Ocean ~)	tayār (m)	تيّار
to surround (bathe)	ḥāṭ	حاط
shore	sāḥel (m)	ساحل
coast	sāḥel (m)	ساحل
flow (flood tide)	tayār (m)	تيّار
ebb (ebb tide)	gozor (m)	جزر
shoal	meyāh ḍaḥla (f)	مياه ضحلة
bottom (~ of the sea)	qāʿ (m)	قاع
wave	mouga (f)	موجة
crest (~ of a wave)	qemma (f)	قمّة
spume (sea foam)	zabad el baḥr (m)	زبد البحر
storm (sea storm)	ʿāṣefa (f)	عاصفة
hurricane	eʿṣār (m)	إعصار
tsunami	tsunāmy (m)	تسونامي
calm (dead ~)	hodūʾ (m)	هدوء
quiet, calm (adj)	hady	هادئ
pole	ʾoṭb (m)	قطب
polar (adj)	ʾoṭby	قطبي
latitude	ʿarḍ (m)	عرض
longitude	χaṭṭ ṭūl (m)	خطّ طول
parallel	motawāz (m)	متواز
equator	χaṭṭ el estewāʾ (m)	خطّ الإستواء
sky	samāʾ (f)	سماء
horizon	ofoq (m)	أفق
air	hawāʾ (m)	هواء
lighthouse	manāra (f)	منارة
to dive (vi)	ɣāṣ	غاص
to sink (ab. boat)	ɣereʾ	غرق
treasures	konūz (pl)	كنوز

78. Seas' and Oceans' names

Atlantic Ocean	el moḥeyṭ el aṭlanṭy (m)	المحيط الأطلنطي
Indian Ocean	el moḥeyṭ el hendy (m)	المحيط الهندي
Pacific Ocean	el moḥeyṭ el hādy (m)	المحيط الهادي
Arctic Ocean	el moḥeyṭ el motagammed el ʃamāly (m)	المحيط المتجمّد الشمالي

Black Sea	el baḥr el aswad (m)	البحر الأسود
Red Sea	el baḥr el aḥmar (m)	البحر الأحمر
Yellow Sea	el baḥr el aṣfar (m)	البحر الأصفر
White Sea	el baḥr el abyaḍ (m)	البحر الأبيض
Caspian Sea	baḥr qazwīn (m)	بحر قزوين
Dead Sea	el baḥr el mayet (m)	البحر الميّت
Mediterranean Sea	el baḥr el abyaḍ el motawasseṭ (m)	البحر الأبيض المتوسّط
Aegean Sea	baḥr eygah (m)	بحر إيجة
Adriatic Sea	el baḥr el adreyatīky (m)	البحر الأدرياتيكي
Arabian Sea	baḥr el ʿarab (m)	بحر العرب
Sea of Japan	baḥr el yabān (m)	بحر اليابان
Bering Sea	baḥr bering (m)	بحر بيرينغ
South China Sea	baḥr el ṣeyn el ganūby (m)	بحر الصين الجنوبي
Coral Sea	baḥr el morgān (m)	بحر المرجان
Tasman Sea	baḥr tazman (m)	بحر تسمان
Caribbean Sea	el baḥr el karību (m)	البحر الكاريبي
Barents Sea	baḥr barents (m)	بحر بارنتس
Kara Sea	baḥr kara (m)	بحر كارا
North Sea	baḥr el ʃamāl (m)	بحر الشمال
Baltic Sea	baḥr el balṭīq (m)	بحر البلطيق
Norwegian Sea	baḥr el nerwīg (m)	بحر النرويج

79. Mountains

mountain	gabal (m)	جبل
mountain range	selselet gebāl (f)	سلسلة جبال
mountain ridge	notūʾ el gabal (m)	نتوء الجبل
summit, top	qemma (f)	قمّة
peak	qemma (f)	قمّة
foot (~ of the mountain)	asfal (m)	أسفل
slope (mountainside)	monḥadar (m)	منحدر
volcano	borkān (m)	بركان
active volcano	borkān naʃeṭ (m)	بركان نشط
dormant volcano	borkān χāmed (m)	بركان خامد
eruption	sawarān (m)	ثوّران
crater	fawhet el borkān (f)	فوهة البركان
magma	magma (f)	ماجما
lava	ḥomam borkāniya (pl)	حمم بركانية
molten (~ lava)	monṣahera	منصهرة
canyon	wādy ḍayeʾ (m)	وادي ضيّق

gorge	mamarr ḍaye' (m)	ممرّ ضيّق
crevice	ʃa'' (m)	شقّ
abyss (chasm)	hāwya (f)	هاوية
pass, col	mamarr gabaly (m)	ممرّ جبلي
plateau	haḍaba (f)	هضبة
cliff	garf (m)	جرف
hill	tall (m)	تلّ
glacier	nahr galīdy (m)	نهر جليدي
waterfall	ʃallāl (m)	شلاّل
geyser	nab' maya ḥāra (m)	نبع ميّة حارة
lake	boḥeyra (f)	بحيرة
plain	sahl (m)	سهل
landscape	manzar ṭabee'y (m)	منظر طبيعي
echo	ṣada (m)	صدى
alpinist	motasalleq el gebāl (m)	متسلّق الجبال
rock climber	motasalleq ṣoxūr (m)	متسلّق صخور
to conquer (in climbing)	taɣallab 'ala	تغلّب على
climb (an easy ~)	tasalloq (m)	تسلّق

80. Mountains names

The Alps	gebāl el alb (pl)	جبال الألب
Mont Blanc	mōn blōn (m)	مون بلون
The Pyrenees	gebāl el barānes (pl)	جبال البرانس
The Carpathians	gebāl el karbāt (pl)	جبال الكاربات
The Ural Mountains	gebāl el urāl (pl)	جبال الأورال
The Caucasus Mountains	gebāl el qoqāz (pl)	جبال القوقاز
Mount Elbrus	gabal elbrus (m)	جبل إلبروس
The Altai Mountains	gebāl altāy (pl)	جبال ألتاي
The Tian Shan	gebāl tian ʃan (pl)	جبال تيان شان
The Pamir Mountains	gebāl bamir (pl)	جبال بامير
The Himalayas	himalāya (pl)	هيمالايا
Mount Everest	gabal everest (m)	جبل افرست
The Andes	gebāl el andīz (pl)	جبال الأنديز
Mount Kilimanjaro	gabal kilimanʒaro (m)	جبل كليمنجارو

81. Rivers

river	nahr (m)	نهر
spring (natural source)	'eyn (m)	عين
riverbed (river channel)	magra el nahr (m)	مجرى النهر

basin (river valley)	ḥoḍe (m)	حوض
to flow into …	ṣabb fe …	...صبّ في
tributary	rāfed (m)	رافد
bank (of river)	ḍaffa (f)	ضفّة
current (stream)	tayār (m)	تيّار
downstream (adv)	ma' ettigāh magra el nahr	مع إتّجاه مجرى النهر
upstream (adv)	ḍed el tayār	ضد التيار
inundation	ɣamr (m)	غمر
flooding	fayaḍān (m)	فيضان
to overflow (vi)	fāḍ	فاض
to flood (vt)	ɣamar	غمر
shallow (shoal)	meyāh ḍaḥla (f)	مياه ضحلة
rapids	monḥadar el nahr (m)	منحدر النهر
dam	sadd (m)	سدّ
canal	qanah (f)	قناة
reservoir (artificial lake)	χazzān mā'y (m)	خزّان مائي
sluice, lock	bawwāba qanṭara (f)	بوّابة قنطرة
water body (pond, etc.)	berka (f)	بركة
swamp (marshland)	mostanqa' (m)	مستنقع
bog, marsh	mostanqa' (m)	مستنقع
whirlpool	dawwāma (f)	دوّامة
stream (brook)	gadwal (m)	جدول
drinking (ab. water)	el ʃorb	الشرب
fresh (~ water)	'azb	عذب
ice	galīd (m)	جليد
to freeze over (ab. river, etc.)	etgammed	إتجمّد

82. Rivers' names

Seine	el seyn (m)	السين
Loire	el lua:r (m)	اللوار
Thames	el teymz (m)	التيمز
Rhine	el rayn (m)	الراين
Danube	el danūb (m)	الدانوب
Volga	el volga (m)	الفولغا
Don	el done (m)	الدون
Lena	lena (m)	لينا
Yellow River	el nahr el aṣfar (m)	النهر الأصفر
Yangtze	el yangesty (m)	اليانغستي

Mekong	el mekong (m)	الميكونغ
Ganges	el ɣang (m)	الغانج
Nile River	el nīl (m)	النيل
Congo River	el kongo (m)	الكونغو
Okavango River	okavango (m)	أوكافانجو
Zambezi River	el zambizi (m)	الزمبيزي
Limpopo River	limbobo (m)	ليمبوبو
Mississippi River	el mississibbi (m)	الميسيسيبي

83. Forest

forest, wood	ɣāba (f)	غابة
forest (as adj)	ɣāba	غابة
thick forest	ɣāba kasīfa (f)	غابة كثيفة
grove	bostān (m)	بستان
forest clearing	ezālet el ɣābāt (f)	إزالة الغابات
thicket	agama (f)	أجمة
scrubland	arāḍy el ʃogayrāt (pl)	أراضي الشجيرات
footpath (troddenpath)	mamarr (m)	ممرّ
gully	wādy ḍaye' (m)	وادي ضيّق
tree	ʃagara (f)	شجرة
leaf	wara'a (f)	ورقة
leaves (foliage)	wara' (m)	ورق
fall of leaves	tasā'oṭ el awrā' (m)	تساقط الأوراق
to fall (ab. leaves)	saqaṭ	سقط
top (of the tree)	ra's (m)	رأس
branch	ɣoṣn (m)	غصن
bough	ɣoṣn ra'īsy (m)	غصن رئيسي
bud (on shrub, tree)	bor'om (m)	برعم
needle (of pine tree)	ʃawka (f)	شوكة
pine cone	kūz el ṣnowbar (m)	كوز الصنوبر
hollow (in a tree)	gofe (m)	جوف
nest	'eʃ (m)	عشّ
burrow (animal hole)	goḥr (m)	جحر
trunk	gez' (m)	جذع
root	gezr (m)	جذر
bark	leḥā' (m)	لحاء
moss	ṭaḥlab (m)	طحلب
to uproot (remove trees or tree stumps)	eqtala'	إقتلع

to chop down	'aṭṭaʿ	قطّع
to deforest (vt)	azāl el ɣabāt	أزال الغابات
tree stump	gezʿ el ʃagara (m)	جذع الشجرة
campfire	nār moχayem (m)	نار مخيّم
forest fire	ḥarī' ɣāba (m)	حريق غابة
to extinguish (vt)	ṭaffa	طفّى
forest ranger	ḥāres el ɣāba (m)	حارس الغابة
protection	ḥemāya (f)	حماية
to protect (~ nature)	ḥama	حمى
poacher	sāre' el ṣeyd (m)	سارق الصيد
steel trap	maṣyada (f)	مصيّدة
to gather, to pick (vt)	gammaʿ	جمّع
to lose one's way	tāh	تاه

84. Natural resources

natural resources	sarawāt ṭabiʿiya (pl)	ثروات طبيعيّة
minerals	maʿāden (pl)	معادن
deposits	rawāseb (pl)	رواسب
field (e.g., oilfield)	ḥaql (m)	حقل
to mine (extract)	estaχrag	إستخرج
mining (extraction)	esteχrāg (m)	إستخراج
ore	χām (m)	خام
mine (e.g., for coal)	mangam (m)	منجم
shaft (mine ~)	mangam (m)	منجم
miner	ʿāmel mangam (m)	عامل منجم
gas (natural ~)	ɣāz (m)	غاز
gas pipeline	χaṭṭ anabīb ɣāz (m)	خطّ أنابيب غاز
oil (petroleum)	nafṭ (m)	نفط
oil pipeline	anabīb el nafṭ (pl)	أنابيب النفط
oil well	bīr el nafṭ (m)	بير النفط
derrick (tower)	ḥaffāra (f)	حفّارة
tanker	nāqelet betrūl (f)	ناقلة بترول
sand	raml (m)	رمل
limestone	ḥagar el kals (m)	حجر الكلس
gravel	ḥaṣa (m)	حصى
peat	χaθ faḥm nabāty (m)	خث فحم نباتي
clay	ṭīn (m)	طين
coal	faḥm (m)	فحم
iron (ore)	ḥadīd (m)	حديد
gold	dahab (m)	ذهب
silver	faḍḍa (f)	فضّة

nickel	nikel (m)	نيكل
copper	neḥās (m)	نحاس
zinc	zink (m)	زنك
manganese	manganīz (m)	منجنيز
mercury	ze'baq (m)	زئبق
lead	roṣāṣ (m)	رصاص
mineral	ma'dan (m)	معدن
crystal	kristāl (m)	كريستال
marble	roχām (m)	رخام
uranium	yuranuim (m)	يورانيوم

85. Weather

weather	ṭa's (m)	طقس
weather forecast	naʃra gawiya (f)	نشرة جويّة
temperature	ḥarāra (f)	حرارة
thermometer	termometr (m)	ترمومتر
barometer	barometr (m)	بارومتر
humid (adj)	roṭob	رطب
humidity	roṭūba (f)	رطوبة
heat (extreme ~)	ḥarāra (f)	حرارة
hot (torrid)	ḥarr	حارّ
it's hot	el gaww ḥarr	الجوّ حرّ
it's warm	el gaww dafa	الجوّ دفا
warm (moderately hot)	dāfe'	دافئ
it's cold	el gaww bāred	الجوّ بارد
cold (adj)	bāred	بارد
sun	ʃams (f)	شمس
to shine (vi)	nawwar	نوّر
sunny (day)	moʃmes	مشمس
to come up (vi)	ʃara'	شرق
to set (vi)	ɣarab	غرب
cloud	saḥāba (f)	سحابة
cloudy (adj)	meɣayem	مغيّم
rain cloud	saḥābet maṭar (f)	سحابة مطر
somber (gloomy)	meɣayem	مغيّم
rain	maṭar (m)	مطر
it's raining	el donia betmaṭṭar	الدنيا بتمطّر
rainy (~ day, weather)	momṭer	ممطر
to drizzle (vi)	maṭṭaret razāz	مطّرت رذاذ
pouring rain	maṭar monhamer (f)	مطر منهمر
downpour	maṭar ɣazīr (m)	مطر غزير

heavy (e.g., ~ rain)	ʃedīd	شديد
puddle	berka (f)	بركة
to get wet (in rain)	ettbal	إتّبل
fog (mist)	ʃabbūra (f)	شبّورة
foggy	fih ʃabbūra	فيه شبّورة
snow	talg (m)	ثلج
it's snowing	fih talg	فيه ثلج

86. Severe weather. Natural disasters

thunderstorm	ʿāṣefa raʿdiya (f)	عاصفة رعدية
lightning (~ strike)	barʾ (m)	برق
to flash (vi)	baraq	برق
thunder	raʿd (m)	رعد
to thunder (vi)	dawa	دوّى
it's thundering	el samāʾ dawat raʿd (f)	السماء دوّت رعد
hail	maṭar bard (m)	مطر برد
it's hailing	maṭṭaret bard	مطّرت برد
to flood (vt)	ɣamar	غمر
flood, inundation	fayaḍān (m)	فيضان
earthquake	zelzāl (m)	زلزال
tremor, quake	hazza arḍiya (f)	هزّة أرضية
epicenter	markaz el zelzāl (m)	مركز الزلزال
eruption	sawarān (m)	ثوّران
lava	ḥomam borkāniya (pl)	حمم بركانية
twister, tornado	eʿṣār (m)	إعصار
typhoon	tyfūn (m)	طوفان
hurricane	eʿṣār (m)	إعصار
storm	ʿāṣefa (f)	عاصفة
tsunami	tsunāmy (m)	تسونامي
cyclone	eʿṣār (m)	إعصار
bad weather	ṭaʾs sayeʾ (m)	طقس سئ
fire (accident)	ḥarīʾ (m)	حريق
disaster	karsa (f)	كارثة
meteorite	nayzek (m)	نيّزك
avalanche	enheyār talgy (m)	إنهيار ثلجي
snowslide	enheyār talgy (m)	إنهيار ثلجي
blizzard	ʿāṣefa talgiya (f)	عاصفة ثلجيّة
snowstorm	ʿāṣefa talgiya (f)	عاصفة ثلجيّة

FAUNA

T&P Books Publishing

87. Mammals. Predators

predator	moftares (m)	مفترس
tiger	nemr (m)	نمر
lion	asad (m)	أسد
wolf	ze'b (m)	ذئب
fox	ta'lab (m)	ثعلب
jaguar	nemr amrīky (m)	نمر أمريكي
leopard	fahd (m)	فهد
cheetah	fahd ṣayād (m)	فهد صيّاد
black panther	nemr aswad (m)	نمر أسوَد
puma	asad el gebāl (m)	أسد الجبال
snow leopard	nemr el tolūg (m)	نمر الثلوج
lynx	waʃaq (m)	وشق
coyote	qayūṭ (m)	قيوط
jackal	ebn 'āwy (m)	ابن آوى
hyena	ḍeb' (m)	ضبع

88. Wild animals

animal	ḥayawān (m)	حيوان
beast (animal)	waḥʃ (m)	وحش
squirrel	sengāb (m)	سنجاب
hedgehog	qonfoz (m)	قنفذ
hare	arnab barry (m)	أرنب برّي
rabbit	arnab (m)	أرنب
badger	ɣarīr (m)	غرير
raccoon	rakūn (m)	راكون
hamster	hamster (m)	هامستر
marmot	marmoṭ (m)	مرموط
mole	χold (m)	خلد
mouse	fār (m)	فأر
rat	gerz (m)	جرذ
bat	χoffāʃ (m)	خفّاش
ermine	qāqem (m)	قاقِم
sable	sammūr (m)	سمّور
marten	fara'īāt (m)	فرائيات

weasel	ebn ʻers (m)	ابن عرس
mink	mink (m)	منك
beaver	qondos (m)	قندس
otter	taʻlab maya (m)	ثعلب الميّة
horse	ḥoṣān (m)	حصان
moose	eyl el mūz (m)	أيّل الموظ
deer	ayl (m)	أيل
camel	gamal (m)	جمل
bison	bison (m)	بيسون
aurochs	byson orobby (m)	بيسون أوروبي
buffalo	gamūs (m)	جاموس
zebra	ḥomār waḥʃy (m)	حمار وحشي
antelope	ẓaby (m)	ظبي
roe deer	yaḥmūr orobby (m)	يحمورأوروبيّ
fallow deer	eyl asmar orobby (m)	أيّل أسمر أوروبي
chamois	ʃamwah (f)	شامواه
wild boar	χenzīr barry (m)	خنزير برّي
whale	ḥūt (m)	حوت
seal	foqma (f)	فقمة
walrus	el kabʻ (m)	الكبع
fur seal	foqmet el farā' (f)	فقمة الفراء
dolphin	dolfīn (m)	دولفين
bear	dobb (m)	دبّ
polar bear	dobb 'oṭṭby (m)	دبّ قطبي
panda	banda (m)	باندا
monkey	'erd (m)	قرد
chimpanzee	ʃimbanzy (m)	شيمبانزي
orangutan	orangutan (m)	أورنغوتان
gorilla	ɣorella (f)	غوريلا
macaque	'erd el makāk (m)	قرد المكاك
gibbon	gibbon (m)	جيبون
elephant	fīl (m)	فيل
rhinoceros	χartīt (m)	خرتيت
giraffe	zarāfa (f)	زرافة
hippopotamus	faras el nahr (m)	فرس النهر
kangaroo	kangarū (m)	كانجّارو
koala (bear)	el koala (m)	الكوالا
mongoose	nems (m)	نمس
chinchilla	ʃenʃīla (f)	شنشيلة
skunk	ẓerbān (m)	ظربان
porcupine	nīṣ (m)	نيص

89. Domestic animals

cat	ʾoṭṭa (f)	قطّة
tomcat	ʾoṭṭ (m)	قطّ
dog	kalb (m)	كلب
horse	ḥoṣān (m)	حصان
stallion (male horse)	χeyl faḥl (m)	خيل فحل
mare	faras (f)	فرس
cow	baʾara (f)	بقرة
bull	sore (m)	ثور
ox	sore (m)	ثور
sheep (ewe)	χarūf (f)	خروف
ram	kebʃ (m)	كبش
goat	meʿza (f)	معزة
billy goat, he-goat	māʿez zakar (m)	ماعز ذكر
donkey	ḥomār (m)	حمار
mule	baɣl (m)	بغل
pig, hog	χenzīr (m)	خنزير
piglet	χannūṣ (m)	خنّوص
rabbit	arnab (m)	أرنب
hen (chicken)	farχa (f)	فرخة
rooster	dīk (m)	ديك
duck	baṭṭa (f)	بطّة
drake	dakar el baṭṭ (m)	ذكر البط
goose	wezza (f)	وزّة
tom turkey, gobbler	dīk rūmy (m)	ديك رومي
turkey (hen)	dīk rūmy (m)	ديك رومي
domestic animals	ḥayawānāt dawāgen (pl)	حيوانات دواجن
tame (e.g., ~ hamster)	alīf	أليف
to tame (vt)	rawweḍ	روّض
to breed (vt)	rabba	ربّى
farm	mazraʿa (f)	مزرعة
poultry	dawāgen (pl)	دواجن
cattle	māʃeya (f)	ماشية
herd (cattle)	qaṭeeʿ (m)	قطيع
stable	esṭabl χeyl (m)	إسطبل خيل
pigpen	ḥazīret χanazīr (f)	حظيرة الخنازير
cowshed	zerībet el baʾar (f)	زريبة البقر
rabbit hutch	qan el arāneb (m)	قن الأرانب
hen house	qan el ferāχ (m)	قن الفراخ

90. Birds

bird	ṭā'er (m)	طائر
pigeon	ḥamāma (f)	حمامة
sparrow	'aṣfūr dawri (m)	عصفور دوري
tit (great tit)	qarqaf (m)	قرقف
magpie	'a''a' (m)	عقعق
raven	ɣorāb aswad (m)	غراب أسود
crow	ɣorāb (m)	غراب
jackdaw	zāɣ zar'y (m)	زاغ زرعي
rook	ɣorāb el qeyẓ (m)	غراب القيظ
duck	baṭṭa (f)	بطّة
goose	wezza (f)	وزّة
pheasant	tadarrog (m)	تدرج
eagle	'eqāb (m)	عقاب
hawk	el bāz (m)	الباز
falcon	ṣa'r (m)	صقر
vulture	nesr (m)	نسر
condor (Andean ~)	kondor (m)	كندور
swan	el temm (m)	التمّ
crane	karkiya (m)	كركية
stork	loqloq (m)	لقلق
parrot	babaɣā' (m)	ببغاء
hummingbird	ṭannān (m)	طنّان
peacock	ṭawūs (m)	طاووس
ostrich	na'āma (f)	نعامة
heron	belʃone (m)	بلشون
flamingo	flamingo (m)	فلامينجو
pelican	bag'a (f)	بجعة
nightingale	'andalīb (m)	عندليب
swallow	el sonūnū (m)	السنونو
thrush	somnet el ḥoqūl (m)	سمنة الحقول
song thrush	somna moɣarreda (m)	سمنة مغرّدة
blackbird	ʃaḥrūr aswad (m)	شحرور أسود
swift	semmāma (m)	سمّامة
lark	qabra (f)	قبرة
quail	semmān (m)	سمّان
woodpecker	na'ār el χaʃab (m)	نقار الخشب
cuckoo	weqwāq (m)	وقواق
owl	būma (f)	بومة
eagle owl	būm orāsy (m)	بوم أوراسي

wood grouse	dīk el χalang (m)	ديك الخلنج
black grouse	ṭyhūg aswad (m)	طيهوج أسوَد
partridge	el ḥagal (m)	الحجل
starling	zerzūr (m)	زرزور
canary	kanāry (m)	كناري
hazel grouse	ṭyhūg el bondo' (m)	طيهوج البندق
chaffinch	ʃarʃūr (m)	شرشور
bullfinch	deɣnāʃ (m)	دغناش
seagull	nawras (m)	نورس
albatross	el qoṭros (m)	القطرس
penguin	beṭrīq (m)	بطريق

91. Fish. Marine animals

bream	abramīs (m)	أبراميس
carp	ʃabbūṭ (m)	شبّوط
perch	farχ (m)	فرخ
catfish	'armūṭ (m)	قرموط
pike	karāky (m)	كراكي
salmon	salamon (m)	سلمون
sturgeon	ḥafʃ (m)	حفش
herring	renga (f)	رنجة
Atlantic salmon	salamon aṭlasy (m)	سلمون أطلسي
mackerel	makerel (m)	ماكريل
flatfish	samak mefalṭah (f)	سمك مفلطح
zander, pike perch	samak sandar (m)	سمك سندر
cod	el qadd (m)	القد
tuna	tuna (f)	تونة
trout	salamon mera''aṭ (m)	سلمون مرقّط
eel	ḥankalīs (m)	حنكليس
electric ray	ra'ād (m)	رعاد
moray eel	moraya (f)	مورايية
piranha	bīrana (f)	بيرانا
shark	'erʃ (m)	قرش
dolphin	dolfīn (m)	دولفين
whale	ḥūt (m)	حوت
crab	kaboria (m)	كابوريا
jellyfish	'andīl el baḥr (m)	قنديل البحر
octopus	aχṭabūṭ (m)	أخطبوط
starfish	negmet el baḥr (f)	نجمة البحر
sea urchin	qonfoz el baḥr (m)	قنفذ البحر

seahorse	ḥoṣān el baḥr (m)	حصان البحر
oyster	maḥār (m)	محار
shrimp	gammbary (m)	جمّبري
lobster	estakoza (f)	استكوزا
spiny lobster	estakoza (m)	استاكوزا

92. Amphibians. Reptiles

snake	teʿbān (m)	ثعبان
venomous (snake)	sām	سام
viper	afʿa (f)	أفعى
cobra	kobra (m)	كوبرا
python	teʿbān byton (m)	ثعبان بايثون
boa	bawāʾ el ʿaṣera (f)	بواء العاصرة
grass snake	teʿbān el ʿoʃb (m)	ثعبان العشب
rattle snake	afʿa megalgela (f)	أفعى مجلجلة
anaconda	anakonda (f)	أناكوندا
lizard	seḥliya (f)	سحليّة
iguana	eɣwana (f)	إغوانة
monitor lizard	warl (m)	ورل
salamander	salamander (m)	سلمندر
chameleon	ḥerbāya (f)	حرباية
scorpion	ʿaʾrab (m)	عقرب
turtle	solḥefah (f)	سلحفاة
frog	ḍeffḍaʿ (m)	ضفدع
toad	ḍeffḍaʿ el ṭeyn (m)	ضفدع الطين
crocodile	temsāḥ (m)	تمساح

93. Insects

insect, bug	ḥaʃara (f)	حشرة
butterfly	farāʃa (f)	فراشة
ant	namla (f)	نملة
fly	debbāna (f)	دبّانة
mosquito	namūsa (f)	ناموسة
beetle	χonfesa (f)	خنفسة
wasp	dabbūr (m)	دبّور
bee	naḥla (f)	نحلة
bumblebee	naḥla ṭannāna (f)	نحلة طنّانة
gadfly (botfly)	naʿra (f)	نعرة
spider	ʿankabūt (m)	عنكبوت
spiderweb	nasīg ʿankabūt (m)	نسيج عنكبوت

dragonfly	ya'sūb (m)	يعسوب
grasshopper	garād (m)	جراد
moth (night butterfly)	'etta (f)	عثّة
cockroach	ṣarṣūr (m)	صرصور
tick	qarāda (f)	قرادة
flea	barɣūt (m)	برغوث
midge	ba'ūḍa (f)	بعوضة
locust	garād (m)	جراد
snail	ḥalazōn (m)	حلزون
cricket	ṣarṣūr el ḥaql (m)	صرصور الحقل
lightning bug	yarā'a (f)	يراعة
ladybug	χonfesa mena'ṭṭa (f)	خنفسة منقّطة
cockchafer	χonfesa motlefa lel nabāt (f)	خنفسة متّلفة للنبات
leech	'alaqa (f)	علقة
caterpillar	yasrū' (m)	يسروع
earthworm	dūda (f)	دودة
larva	yaraqa (f)	يرقة

FLORA

T&P Books Publishing

94. Trees

tree	ʃagara (f)	شجرة
deciduous (adj)	nafḍiya	نفضيّة
coniferous (adj)	ṣonoberiya	صنوبرية
evergreen (adj)	dāʾemet el χoḍra	دائمة الخضرة
apple tree	ʃagaret toffāḥ (f)	شجرة تفّاح
pear tree	ʃagaret komettra (f)	شجرة كمثّرى
cherry tree	ʃagaret karaz (f)	شجرة كرز
plum tree	ʃagaret barʾūʾ (f)	شجرة برقوق
birch	batola (f)	بتولا
oak	ballūṭ (f)	بلّوط
linden tree	zayzafūn (f)	زيزفون
aspen	ḥūr rāgef	حور راجف
maple	qayqab (f)	قيقب
spruce	rateng (f)	راتينج
pine	ṣonober (f)	صنوبر
larch	arziya (f)	أرزية
fir tree	tanūb (f)	تنوب
cedar	el orz (f)	الأرز
poplar	ḥūr (f)	حور
rowan	ɣobayrāʾ (f)	غبيراء
willow	ṣefsāf (f)	صفصاف
alder	gār el māʾ (m)	جار الماء
beech	el zān (f)	الزان
elm	derdar (f)	دردار
ash (tree)	marān (f)	مران
chestnut	kastanāʾ (f)	كستناء
magnolia	maɣnolia (f)	ماغنوليا
palm tree	naχla (f)	نخلة
cypress	el soro (f)	السرو
mangrove	mangrūf (f)	مانجروف
baobab	baobab (f)	باوباب
eucalyptus	eukalyptus (f)	أوكالبتوس
sequoia	sequoia (f)	سيكويا

95. Shrubs

bush	ʃogeyra (f)	شجيرة
shrub	ʃogayrāt (pl)	شجيرات
grapevine	karma (f)	كرمة
vineyard	karam (m)	كرم
raspberry bush	zar'et tūt el 'alī' el aḥmar (f)	زرعة توت العليق الأحمر
redcurrant bush	keʃmeʃ aḥmar (m)	كشمش أحمر
gooseberry bush	'enab el sa'lab (m)	عنب الثعلب
acacia	aqaqia (f)	أقاقيا
barberry	berbarīs (m)	برباريس
jasmine	yasmīn (m)	ياسمين
juniper	'ar'ar (m)	عرعر
rosebush	ʃogeyret ward (f)	شجيرة ورد
dog rose	ward el seyāg (pl)	ورد السياج

96. Fruits. Berries

fruit	tamra (f)	تمرة
fruits	tamr (m)	تمر
apple	toffāḥa (f)	تفّاحة
pear	komettra (f)	كمّثرى
plum	bar'ū' (m)	برقوق
strawberry (garden ~)	farawla (f)	فراولة
cherry	karaz (m)	كرز
grape	'enab (m)	عنب
raspberry	tūt el 'alī' el aḥmar (m)	توت العليق الأحمر
blackcurrant	keʃmeʃ aswad (m)	كشمش أسود
redcurrant	keʃmeʃ aḥmar (m)	كشمش أحمر
gooseberry	'enab el sa'lab (m)	عنب الثعلب
cranberry	'enabiya ḥāda el χebā' (m)	عنبية حادة الخباء
orange	bortoqāl (m)	برتقال
mandarin	yosfy (m)	يوسفي
pineapple	ananās (m)	أناناس
banana	moze (m)	موز
date	tamr (m)	تمر
lemon	lymūn (m)	ليمون
apricot	meʃmeʃ (f)	مشمش
peach	χawχa (f)	خوخة
kiwi	kiwi (m)	كيوي
grapefruit	grabe frūt (m)	جريب فروت

berry	tūt (m)	توت
berries	tūt (pl)	توت
cowberry	ʿenab el sore (m)	عنب الثور
wild strawberry	farawla barriya (f)	فراولة بريّة
bilberry	ʿenab al aḥrāg (m)	عنب الأحراج

97. Flowers. Plants

flower	zahra (f)	زهرة
bouquet (of flowers)	bokeyh (f)	بوكيه
rose (flower)	warda (f)	وردة
tulip	tolīb (f)	توليب
carnation	ʾoronfol (m)	قرنفل
gladiolus	el dalbūs (f)	الدّلَبُوثُ
cornflower	qanṭeryūn ʿanbary (m)	قنطريون عنبري
harebell	garīs mostadīr el awrāʾ (m)	جريس مستدير الأوراق
dandelion	handabāʾ (f)	هندباء
camomile	kamomile (f)	كاموميل
aloe	el alowa (m)	الألوّة
cactus	ṣabbār (m)	صبّار
rubber plant, ficus	faykas (m)	فيكس
lily	zanbaq (f)	زنبق
geranium	ɣarnūqy (f)	غرنوقي
hyacinth	el lavender (f)	اللافندر
mimosa	mimoza (f)	ميموزا
narcissus	nerges (f)	نرجس
nasturtium	abo χangar (f)	أبو خنجر
orchid	orkid (f)	أوركيد
peony	fawnia (f)	فاوانيا
violet	el banafseg (f)	البنفسج
pansy	bansy (f)	بانسي
forget-me-not	ʾāzān el faʾr (pl)	آذان الفأر
daisy	aqwaḥān (f)	أقحوان
poppy	el χoʃχāʃ (f)	الخشخاش
hemp	qanb (m)	قنب
mint	neʿnāʿ (m)	نعناع
lily of the valley	zanbaq el wādy (f)	زنبق الوادي
snowdrop	zahrat el laban (f)	زهرة اللبن
nettle	ʾarrāṣ (m)	قرّاص
sorrel	ḥammāḍ bostāny (m)	حمّاض بستاني

water lily	niloferiya (f)	نيلوفرية
fern	sarxas (m)	سرخس
lichen	aʃna (f)	أشنة
greenhouse (tropical ~)	ṣoba (f)	صوبة
lawn	ʿoʃb axḍar (m)	عشب أخضر
flowerbed	geneynet zohūr (f)	جنينة زهور
plant	nabāt (m)	نبات
grass	ʿoʃb (m)	عشب
blade of grass	ʿoʃba (f)	عشبة
leaf	waraʾa (f)	ورقة
petal	waraʾet el zahra (f)	ورقة الزهرة
stem	sāq (f)	ساق
tuber	darna (f)	درنة
young plant (shoot)	nabta saɣīra (f)	نبتة صغيرة
thorn	ʃawka (f)	شوكة
to blossom (vi)	fattaḥet	فتّحت
to fade, to wither	debel	ذبل
smell (odor)	rīḥa (f)	ريحة
to cut (flowers)	ʾaṭaʿ	قطع
to pick (a flower)	ʾaṭaf	قطف

98. Cereals, grains

grain	ḥobūb (pl)	حبوب
cereal crops	maḥaṣīl el ḥubūb (pl)	محاصيل الحبوب
ear (of barley, etc.)	sonbola (f)	سنبلة
wheat	ʾamḥ (m)	قمح
rye	ʃelm mazrūʿ (m)	شيلم مزروع
oats	ʃofān (m)	شوفان
millet	el dexn (m)	الدخن
barley	ʃeʿīr (m)	شعير
corn	dora (f)	ذرة
rice	rozz (m)	رزّ
buckwheat	ḥanṭa sodaʾ (f)	حنطة سوداء
pea plant	besella (f)	بسلّة
kidney bean	faṣolya (f)	فاصوليا
soy	fūl el ṣoya (m)	فول الصويا
lentil	ʿads (m)	عدس
beans (pulse crops)	fūl (m)	فول

T&P BOOKS

COUNTRIES OF THE WORLD

T&P Books Publishing

99. Countries. Part 1

Afghanistan	afɣanistan (f)	أفغانستان
Albania	albānia (f)	ألبانيا
Argentina	arʒantīn (f)	الأرجنتين
Armenia	armīnia (f)	أرمينيا
Australia	ostorālya (f)	أستراليا
Austria	el nemsa (f)	النمسا
Azerbaijan	azrabiʒān (m)	أذربيجان
The Bahamas	gozor el bahāmas (pl)	جزر البهاماس
Bangladesh	bangladeʃ (f)	بنجلاديش
Belarus	belarūsia (f)	بيلاروسيا
Belgium	balʒīka (f)	بلجيكا
Bolivia	bolivia (f)	بوليفيا
Bosnia and Herzegovina	el bosna wel harsek (f)	البوسنة والهرسك
Brazil	el barazīl (f)	البرازيل
Bulgaria	bolɣāria (f)	بلغاريا
Cambodia	kambodya (f)	كمبوديا
Canada	kanada (f)	كندا
Chile	tʃīly (f)	تشيلي
China	el ṣīn (f)	الصين
Colombia	kolombia (f)	كولومبيا
Croatia	kroātya (f)	كرواتيا
Cuba	kūba (f)	كوبا
Cyprus	ʾobroṣ (f)	قبرص
Czech Republic	gomhoriya el tʃīk (f)	جمهورية التشيك
Denmark	el denmark (f)	الدنمارك
Dominican Republic	gomhoriya el dominikan (f)	جمهوريّة الدومينيكان
Ecuador	el equador (f)	الإكوادور
Egypt	maṣr (f)	مصر
England	engeltera (f)	إنجلّترا
Estonia	estūnia (f)	إستونيا
Finland	finlanda (f)	فنّلندا
France	faransa (f)	فرنسا
French Polynesia	bolenezia el faransiya (f)	بولينزيا الفرنسيّة
Georgia	ʒorʒia (f)	جورجيا
Germany	almānya (f)	ألمانيا
Ghana	ɣana (f)	غانا
Great Britain	briṭaniya el ʿozma (f)	بريطانيا العظمى
Greece	el yunān (f)	اليونان
Haiti	haīti (f)	هايتي
Hungary	el magar (f)	المجر

100. Countries. Part 2

Iceland	'āyslanda (f)	آيسلندا
India	el hend (f)	الهند
Indonesia	indonisya (f)	إندونيسيا
Iran	iran (f)	إيران
Iraq	el 'erāq (m)	العراق
Ireland	irelanda (f)	أيرلندا
Israel	isra'īl (f)	إسرائيل
Italy	eṭālia (f)	إيطاليا
Jamaica	ʒamayka (f)	جامايكا
Japan	el yabān (f)	اليابان
Jordan	el ordon (m)	الأردن
Kazakhstan	kazaχistān (f)	كازاخستّان
Kenya	kenya (f)	كينيا
Kirghizia	qirɣizestān (f)	قيرغيزستان
Kuwait	el kuweyt (f)	الكويت
Laos	laos (f)	لاوس
Latvia	latvia (f)	لاتفيا
Lebanon	lebnān (f)	لبنان
Libya	libya (f)	ليبيا
Liechtenstein	liʃtenʃtayn (m)	ليشتنشتاين
Lithuania	litwānia (f)	ليتوانيا
Luxembourg	luksemburg (f)	لوكسمبورج
Macedonia (Republic of ~)	maqdūnia (f)	مقدونيا
Madagascar	madaɣaʃkar (f)	مدغشقر
Malaysia	malīzya (f)	ماليزيا
Malta	malṭa (f)	مالطا
Mexico	el maksīk (f)	المكسيك
Moldova, Moldavia	moldāvia (f)	مولدافيا
Monaco	monako (f)	موناكو
Mongolia	manɣūlia (f)	منغوليا
Montenegro	el gabal el aswad (m)	الجبل الأسوّد
Morocco	el maɣreb (m)	المغرب
Myanmar	myanmar (f)	ميانمار
Namibia	namibia (f)	ناميبيا
Nepal	nebāl (f)	نيبال
Netherlands	holanda (f)	هولندا
New Zealand	nyu zelanda (f)	نيوزيلنّدا
North Korea	korea el ʃamāliya (f)	كوريا الشماليّة
Norway	el nerwīg (f)	النرويج

101. Countries. Part 3

Pakistan	bakistān (f)	باكستان
Palestine	felesṭīn (f)	فلسطين

Panama	banama (f)	بنما
Paraguay	baraguay (f)	باراجواي
Peru	beru (f)	بيرو
Poland	bolanda (f)	بولندا
Portugal	el bortoɣāl (f)	البرتغال
Romania	romānia (f)	رومانيا
Russia	rūsya (f)	روسيا
Saudi Arabia	el soʿodiya (f)	السعوديّة
Scotland	oskotlanda (f)	اسكتّلندا
Senegal	el senɣāl (f)	السنغال
Serbia	ṣerbia (f)	صربيا
Slovakia	slovākia (f)	سلوفاكيا
Slovenia	slovenia (f)	سلوفينيا
South Africa	afreqia el ganūbiya (f)	أفريقيا الجنوبيّة
South Korea	korea el ganūbiya (f)	كوريا الجنوبيّة
Spain	asbānya (f)	إسبانيا
Suriname	surinam (f)	سورينام
Sweden	el sweyd (f)	السويد
Switzerland	swesra (f)	سويسرا
Syria	soria (f)	سوريا
Taiwan	taywān (f)	تايوان
Tajikistan	ṭaʒīkistan (f)	طاجيكستان
Tanzania	tanznia (f)	تنزانيا
Tasmania	tasmania (f)	تاسمانيا
Thailand	tayland (f)	تايلاند
Tunisia	tunis (f)	تونس
Turkey	turkia (f)	تركيا
Turkmenistan	turkmānistān (f)	تركمانستان
Ukraine	okrānia (f)	أوكرانيا
United Arab Emirates	el emārāt el ʿarabiya el mottaḥeda (pl)	الإمارات العربية المتّحدة
United States of America	el welayāt el mottaḥda el amrīkiya (pl)	الولايات المتّحدة الأمريكيّة
Uruguay	uruguay (f)	أوروجواي
Uzbekistan	uzbakistān (f)	أوزبكستان
Vatican	el vatikān (m)	الفاتيكان
Venezuela	venzweyla (f)	فنزويلا
Vietnam	vietnām (f)	فيتنام
Zanzibar	zanʒibār (f)	زنجبار

GASTRONOMIC GLOSSARY

This section contains a lot of words and terms associated with food. This dictionary will make it easier for you to understand the menu at a restaurant and choose the right dish

T&P Books Publishing

English-Egyptian Arabic gastronomic glossary

aftertaste	ṭaʿm ma baʿd el mazāq (m)	طعم ما بعد المذاق
almond	loze (m)	لوز
anise	yansūn (m)	ينسون
aperitif	ʃarāb (m)	شراب
appetite	ʃahiya (f)	شهيّة
appetizer	moqabbelāt (pl)	مقبّلات
apple	toffāḥa (f)	تفّاحة
apricot	meʃmeʃ (f)	مشمش
artichoke	χarʃūf (m)	خرشوف
asparagus	helione (m)	هليون
Atlantic salmon	salamon aṭlasy (m)	سلمون أطلسي
avocado	avokado (f)	افوكاتو
bacon	bakon (m)	بيكون
banana	moze (m)	موز
barley	ʃeʿīr (m)	شعير
bartender	bārman (m)	بارمان
basil	rīḥān (m)	ريحان
bay leaf	wara' el ɣār (m)	ورق الغار
beans	fūl (m)	فول
beef	laḥm baqary (m)	لحم بقري
beer	bīra (f)	بيرة
beetroot	bangar (m)	بنجر
bell pepper	felfel (m)	فلفل
berries	tūt (pl)	توت
berry	tūt (m)	توت
bilberry	ʿenab al aḥrāg (m)	عنب الأحراج
birch bolete	feṭr boleṭe (m)	فطر بوليط
bitter	morr	مرّ
black coffee	'ahwa sāda (f)	قهوة سادة
black pepper	felfel aswad (m)	فلفل أسوّد
black tea	ʃāy aḥmar (m)	شاي أحمر
blackberry	tūt aswad (m)	توت أسود
blackcurrant	keʃmeʃ aswad (m)	كشمش أسود
boiled	maslū'	مسلوق
bottle opener	fattāḥa (f)	فتّاحة
bread	ʿeyʃ (m)	عيش
breakfast	foṭūr (m)	فطور
bream	abramīs (m)	أبراميس
broccoli	brokkoli (m)	بركولي
Brussels sprouts	koronb broksel (m)	كرنب بروكسل
buckwheat	ḥanṭa soda' (f)	حنطة سوداء
butter	zebda (f)	زبّدة
buttercream	krīmet zebda (f)	كريمة زبدة
cabbage	koronb (m)	كرنب

cake	keyka (f)	كيكة
cake	torta (f)	تورتة
calorie	so'ra ḥarāriya (f)	سعرة حراريّة
can opener	fattāḥa (f)	فتّاحة
candy	bonbony (m)	بونبوني
canned food	mo'allabāt (pl)	معلّبات
cappuccino	kaputʃino (m)	كابتشينو
caraway	karawya (f)	كراوية
carbohydrates	naʃawīāt (pl)	نشويّات
carbonated	kanz	كانز
carp	ʃabbūṭ (m)	شبّوط
carrot	gazar (m)	جزر
catfish	'armūṭ (m)	قرموط
cauliflower	'arnabīṭ (m)	قرنبيط
caviar	kaviar (m)	كافيار
celery	karfas (m)	كرفس
cep	feṭr boleṭe ma'kūl (m)	فطر بوليط مأكول
cereal crops	maḥaṣīl el ḥubūb (pl)	محاصيل الحبوب
cereal grains	ḥobūb 'amḥ (pl)	حبوب قمح
champagne	ʃambania (f)	شمبانيا
chanterelle	feṭr el ʃanterel (m)	فطر الشانتريل
check	ḥesāb (m)	حساب
cheese	gebna (f)	جبنة
chewing gum	lebān (m)	لبان
chicken	ferāχ (m)	فراخ
chocolate	ʃokolāta (f)	شكولاتة
chocolate	bel ʃokolāṭa	بالشكولاتة
cinnamon	'erfa (f)	قرفة
clear soup	mara'a (m)	مرقة
cloves	'oronfol (m)	قرنفل
cocktail	koktayl (m)	كوكتيل
coconut	goze el hend (m)	جوز هند
cod	samak el qadd (m)	سمك القد
coffee	'ahwa (f)	قهوة
coffee with milk	'ahwa bel ḥalīb (f)	قهوة بالحليب
cognac	konyāk (m)	كونياك
cold	bāred	بارد
condensed milk	ḥalīb mokassaf (m)	حليب مكثّف
condiment	bahār (m)	بهار
confectionery	ḥalawīāt (pl)	حلويّات
cookies	baskawīt (m)	بسكويت
coriander	kozbora (f)	كزبرة
corkscrew	barrīma (f)	بريمة
corn	dora (f)	ذرة
corn	dora (f)	ذرة
cornflakes	korn fleks (m)	كورن فليكس
course, dish	wagba (f)	وجبة
cowberry	'enab el sore (m)	عنب الثور
crab	kaboria (m)	كابوريا
cranberry	'enabiya ḥāda el χebā' (m)	عنبية حادة الخباء
cream	krīma (f)	كريمة
crumb	fattāta (f)	فتاتة

cucumber	χeyār (m)	خيار
cuisine	maṭbaχ (m)	مطبخ
cup	fengān (m)	فنجان
dark beer	bīra ɣam'a (f)	بيرة غامقة
date	tamr (m)	تمر
death cap	feṭr amanīt falusyāny el sām (m)	فطر أمانيت فالوسياني السام
dessert	ḥalawīāt (pl)	حلويّات
diet	reʒīm (m)	رجيم
dill	ʃabat (m)	شبت
dinner	ʿaʃā' (m)	عشاء
dried	mogaffaf	مجفّف
drinking water	mayet ʃorb (m)	ميّة شرب
duck	baṭṭa (f)	بطّة
ear	sonbola (f)	سنبلة
edible mushroom	feṭr ṣāleḥ lel akl (m)	فطر صالح للأكل
eel	ḥankalīs (m)	حنكليس
egg	beyḍa (f)	بيضة
egg white	bayāḍ el beyḍ (m)	بياض البيض
egg yolk	ṣafār el beyḍ (m)	صفار البيض
eggplant	bātengān (m)	باذنجان
eggs	beyḍ (m)	بيض
Enjoy your meal!	bel hana wel ʃefa!	بالهنا والشفا!
fats	dohūn (pl)	دهون
fig	tīn (m)	تين
filling	ḥaʃwa (f)	حشوة
fish	samak (m)	سمك
flatfish	samak mefalṭah (f)	سمك مفلطح
flour	de'ī' (m)	دقيق
fly agaric	feṭr amanīt el ṭā'er (m)	فطر أمانيت الطائر
food	akl (m)	أكل
fork	ʃawka (f)	شوكة
freshly squeezed juice	ʿaṣīr freʃ (m)	عصير فريش
fried	ma'ly	مقلي
fried eggs	beyḍ ma'ly (m)	بيض مقلي
frozen	mogammad	مجمّد
fruit	faχa (f)	فاكهة
fruits	tamr (m)	تمر
game	ṣeyd (m)	صيد
gammon	faχd χanzīr (m)	فخد خنزير
garlic	tūm (m)	ثوم
gin	ʒin (m)	جين
ginger	zangabīl (m)	زنجبيل
glass	kobbāya (f)	كوبّاية
glass	kāsa (f)	كاسة
goose	wezza (f)	وزّة
gooseberry	ʿenab el saʿlab (m)	عنب الثعلب
grain	ḥobūb (pl)	حبوب
grape	ʿenab (m)	عنب
grapefruit	grabe frūt (m)	جريب فروت
green tea	ʃāy aχḍar (m)	شاي أخضر
greens	χoḍrawāt waraqiya (pl)	خضروات ورقية

halibut	samak el halbūt (m)	سمك الهلبوت
ham	hām(m)	هام
hamburger	hamburger (m)	هامبورجر
hamburger	hamburger (m)	هامبورجر
hazelnut	bondo' (m)	بندق
herring	renga (f)	رنجة
honey	'asal (m)	عسل
horseradish	fegl ḥār (m)	فجل حار
hot	soχn	سخن
ice	talg (m)	ثلج
ice-cream	'ays krīm (m)	آيس كريم
instant coffee	neskafe (m)	نيسكافيه
jam	mrabba (m)	مربّى
jam	mrabba (m)	مربّى
juice	'aṣīr (m)	عصير
kidney bean	faṣolya (f)	فاصوليا
kiwi	kiwi (m)	كيوي
knife	sekkīna (f)	سكّينة
lamb	laḥm ḍāny (m)	لحم ضاني
lemon	lymūn (m)	ليمون
lemonade	limonāta (f)	ليموناتة
lentil	'ads (m)	عدس
lettuce	χass (m)	خسّ
light beer	bīra χafīfa (f)	بيرة خفيفة
liqueur	liqure (m)	ليكيور
liquors	maʃrūbāt koḥūliya (pl)	مشروبات كحولية
liver	kebda (f)	كبدة
lunch	ɣada' (m)	غداء
mackerel	makerel (m)	ماكريل
mandarin	yosfy (m)	يوسفي
mango	manga (m)	مانجة
margarine	margarīn (m)	مارجرين
marmalade	marmalād (f)	مرملاد
mashed potatoes	baṭāṭes mahrūsa (f)	بطاطس مهروسة
mayonnaise	mayonnɛ:z (m)	مايونيز
meat	laḥma (f)	لحمة
melon	ʃammām (f)	شمّام
menu	qā'emet el ṭa'ām (f)	قائمة طعام
milk	laban (m)	لبن
milkshake	milk ʃejk (m)	ميلك شيك
millet	el deχn (m)	الدُخن
mineral water	maya ma'daniya (f)	ميّة معدنية
morel	feṭr el ɣoʃna (m)	فطر الغوشنة
mushroom	feṭr (f)	فطر
mustard	mosṭarda (m)	مسطردة
non-alcoholic	men ɣeyr koḥūl	من غير كحول
noodles	nūdles (f)	نودلز
oats	ʃofān (m)	شوفان
olive oil	zeyt el zaytūn (m)	زيت الزيتون
olives	zaytūn (m)	زيتون
omelet	omlette (m)	اومليت
onion	baṣal (m)	بصل

orange	bortoqāl (m)	برتقال
orange juice	ʿaṣīr bortoqāl (m)	عصير برتقال
orange-cap boletus	feṭr aḥmar (m)	فطر أحمر
oyster	maḥār (m)	محار
pâté	maʿgūn laḥm (m)	معجون لحم
papaya	babāya (m)	ببايا
paprika	babrika (f)	بابريكا
parsley	baʾdūnes (m)	بقدونس
pasta	makaruna (f)	مكرونة
pea	besella (f)	بسلّة
peach	χawχa (f)	خوخة
peanut	fūl sudāny (m)	فول سوداني
pear	komettra (f)	كمّثرى
peel	ʾeʃra (f)	قشرة
perch	farχ (m)	فرخ
pickled	meχallel	مخلّل
pie	feṭīra (f)	فطيرة
piece	ʾeṭʿa (f)	قطعة
pike	samak el karāky (m)	سمك الكراكي
pike perch	samak sandar (m)	سمك سندر
pineapple	ananās (m)	أناناس
pistachios	fostoʾ (m)	فستق
pizza	bītza (f)	بيتزا
plate	ṭabaʾ (m)	طبق
plum	barʾūʾ (m)	برقوق
poisonous mushroom	feṭr sām (m)	فطر سام
pomegranate	rommān (m)	رمان
pork	laḥm el χanazīr (m)	لحم الخنزير
porridge	ʿaṣīda (f)	عصيدة
portion	naṣīb (m)	نصيب
potato	baṭāṭes (f)	بطاطس
proteins	brotenāt (pl)	بروتينات
pub, bar	bār (m)	بار
pudding	būding (m)	بودنج
pumpkin	qarʿ ʿasaly (m)	قرع عسلي
rabbit	laḥm arāneb (m)	لحم أرانب
radish	fegl (m)	فجل
raisin	zebīb (m)	زبيب
raspberry	tūt el ʿalīʾ el aḥmar (m)	توت العليق الأحمر
recipe	waṣfa (f)	وصفة
red pepper	felfel aḥmar (m)	فلفل أحمر
red wine	nebī aḥmar (m)	نبيذ أحمر
redcurrant	keʃmeʃ aḥmar (m)	كشمش أحمر
refreshing drink	ḥāga saʾʿa (f)	حاجة ساقعة
rice	rozz (m)	رزّ
rum	rum (m)	رم
russula	feṭr russula (m)	فطر روسولا
rye	ʃelm mazrūʿ (m)	شيلم مزروع
saffron	zaʿfarān (m)	زعفران
salad	solṭa (f)	سلطة
salmon	salamon (m)	سلمون
salt	melḥ (m)	ملح

salty	māleḥ	مالح
sandwich	sandawitʃ (m)	ساندويتش
sardine	sardīn (m)	سردين
sauce	ṣalṣa (f)	صلصة
saucer	ṭaba' fengān (m)	طبق فنجان
sausage	sogo'' (m)	سجق
seafood	sīfūd (pl)	سي فود
sesame	semsem (m)	سمسم
shark	'erʃ (m)	قرش
shrimp	gammbary (m)	جمّبري
side dish	ṭaba' gāneby (m)	طبق جانبي
slice	ʃarīḥa (f)	شريحة
smoked	modakχen	مدخّن
soft drink	maʃrūb ɣāzy (m)	مشروب غازي
soup	ʃorba (f)	شوربة
soup spoon	maʿla'a kebīra (f)	ملعقة كبيرة
sour cream	kreyma ḥamḍa (f)	كريمة حامضة
soy	fūl el ṣoya (m)	فول الصويا
spaghetti	spaɣetti (m)	سباجيتي
sparkling	kanz	كانز
spice	bahār (m)	بهار
spinach	sabāneχ (m)	سبانخ
spiny lobster	estakoza (m)	استاكوزا
spoon	maʿla'a (f)	معلقة
squid	kalmāry (m)	كالماري
steak	steak laḥm (m)	ستيك لحم
still	rakeda	راكدة
strawberry	farawla (f)	فراولة
sturgeon	samak el ḥafʃ (m)	سمك الحفش
sugar	sokkar (m)	سكّر
sunflower oil	zeyt ʿabbād el ʃams (m)	زيت عبّاد الشمس
sweet	mesakkar	مسكّر
taste, flavor	ṭaʿm (m)	طعم
tasty	ḥelw	حلو
tea	ʃāy (m)	شاي
teaspoon	maʿla'et ʃāy (f)	معلقة شاي
tip	ba'ʃīʃ (m)	بقشيش
tomato	ṭamāṭem (f)	طماطم
tomato juice	ʿaṣīr ṭamāṭem (m)	عصير طماطم
tongue	lesān (m)	لسان
toothpick	χallet senān (f)	خلة سنان
trout	salamon mera''aṭ (m)	سلمون مرقّط
tuna	tuna (f)	تونة
turkey	dīk rūmy (m)	ديك رومي
turnip	left (m)	لفت
veal	laḥm el ʿegl (m)	لحم العجل
vegetable oil	zeyt (m)	زيت
vegetables	χoḍār (pl)	خضار
vegetarian	nabāty (m)	نباتي
vegetarian	nabāty	نباتي
vermouth	vermote (m)	فيرموت
vienna sausage	sogo'' (m)	سجق

vinegar	χall (m)	خلّ
vitamin	vitamīn (m)	فيتامين
vodka	vodka (f)	فودكا
waffles	waffles (pl)	وافلز
waiter	garsone (m)	جرسون
waitress	garsona (f)	جرسونة
walnut	'eyn gamal (f)	عين الجمل
water	meyāh (f)	مياه
watermelon	baṭṭīχ (m)	بطّيخ
wheat	'amḥ (m)	قمح
whiskey	wiski (m)	ويسكي
white wine	nebīz abyaḍ (m)	نبيذ أبيض
wild strawberry	farawla barriya (f)	فراولة برّيّة
wine	χamra (f)	خمرة
wine list	qā'emet el χomūr (f)	قائمة خمور
with ice	bel talg	بالتلج
yogurt	zabādy (m)	زبادي
zucchini	kōsa (f)	كوسة

Egyptian Arabic-English gastronomic glossary

بالهنا والشفا!	bel hana wel ʃefa!	Enjoy your meal!
آيس كريم	'ays krīm (m)	ice-cream
أبراميس	abramīs (m)	bream
أكل	akl (m)	food
أناناس	ananās (m)	pineapple
استاكوزا	estakoza (m)	spiny lobster
افوكاتو	avokado (f)	avocado
الدُخن	el deχn (m)	millet
اومليت	omlette (m)	omelet
بابريكا	babrika (f)	paprika
باذنجان	bātengān (m)	eggplant
بار	bār (m)	pub, bar
بارد	bāred	cold
بارمان	bārman (m)	bartender
بالتلج	bel talg	with ice
بالشكولاتة	bel ʃokolāṭa	chocolate
بابايا	babāya (m)	papaya
برتقال	bortoqāl (m)	orange
برقوق	bar'ū' (m)	plum
بركولي	brokkoli (m)	broccoli
بروتينات	brotenāt (pl)	proteins
بريّمة	barrīma (f)	corkscrew
بسكويت	baskawīt (m)	cookies
بسلّة	besella (f)	pea
بصل	baṣal (m)	onion
بطاطس	baṭāṭes (f)	potato
بطاطس مهروسة	baṭāṭes mahrūsa (f)	mashed potatoes
بطّة	baṭṭa (f)	duck
بطّيخ	baṭṭīχ (m)	watermelon
بقدونس	ba'dūnes (m)	parsley
بقشيش	ba'ʃīʃ (m)	tip
بنجر	bangar (m)	beetroot
بندق	bondo' (m)	hazelnut
بهار	bahār (m)	condiment
بهار	bahār (m)	spice
بودنج	būding (m)	pudding
بونبوني	bonbony (m)	candy
بياض البيض	bayāḍ el beyḍ (m)	egg white
بيتزا	bītza (f)	pizza
بيرة	bīra (f)	beer
بيرة خفيفة	bīra χafīfa (f)	light beer
بيرة غامقة	bīra ɣam'a (f)	dark beer
بيض	beyḍ (m)	eggs
بيض مقلي	beyḍ ma'ly (m)	fried eggs

بيضة	beyḍa (f)	egg
بيكون	bakon (m)	bacon
تفّاحة	toffāḥa (f)	apple
تمر	tamr (m)	date
تمر	tamr (m)	fruits
توت	tūt (m)	berry
توت	tūt (pl)	berries
توت أسود	tūt aswad (m)	blackberry
توت العليق الأحمر	tūt el ʿalīʾ el aḥmar (m)	raspberry
تورتة	torta (f)	cake
تونة	tuna (f)	tuna
تين	tīn (m)	fig
ثلج	talg (m)	ice
ثوم	tūm (m)	garlic
جبنة	gebna (f)	cheese
جرسون	garsone (m)	waiter
جرسونة	garsona (f)	waitress
جريب فروت	grabe frūt (m)	grapefruit
جزر	gazar (m)	carrot
جمّبري	gammbary (m)	shrimp
جوز هند	goze el hend (m)	coconut
جين	ʒin (m)	gin
حاجة ساقعة	ḥāga saʾʿa (f)	refreshing drink
حبوب	ḥobūb (pl)	grain
حبوب قمح	ḥobūb ʾamḥ (pl)	cereal grains
حساب	ḥesāb (m)	check
حشوة	ḥaʃwa (f)	filling
حلو	ḥelw	tasty
حلويّات	ḥalawīāt (pl)	confectionery
حلويّات	ḥalawīāt (pl)	dessert
حليب مكثّف	ḥalīb mokassaf (m)	condensed milk
حنطة سوداء	ḥanṭa sodaʾ (f)	buckwheat
حنكليس	ḥankalīs (m)	eel
خرشوف	χarʃūf (m)	artichoke
خسّ	χass (m)	lettuce
خضار	χoḍār (pl)	vegetables
خضروات ورقية	χoḍrawāt waraqiya (pl)	greens
خلة سنان	χallet senān (f)	toothpick
خلّ	χall (m)	vinegar
خمرة	χamra (f)	wine
خوخة	χawχa (f)	peach
خيار	χeyār (m)	cucumber
دقيق	deʾīʾ (m)	flour
دهون	dohūn (pl)	fats
ديك رومي	dīk rūmy (m)	turkey
ذرة	dora (f)	corn
ذرة	dora (f)	corn
راكدة	rakeda	still
رجيم	reʒīm (m)	diet
رزّ	rozz (m)	rice
رم	rum (m)	rum
رمان	rommān (m)	pomegranate

رنجة	renga (f)	herring
ريحان	rīḥān (m)	basil
زبادي	zabādy (m)	yogurt
زبيب	zebīb (m)	raisin
زبدة	zebda (f)	butter
زعفران	za'farān (m)	saffron
زنجبيل	zangabīl (m)	ginger
زيت	zeyt (m)	vegetable oil
زيت الزيتون	zeyt el zaytūn (m)	olive oil
زيت عبّاد الشمس	zeyt 'abbād el ʃams (m)	sunflower oil
زيتون	zaytūn (m)	olives
ساندويتش	sandawitʃ (m)	sandwich
سباجيتي	spaɣetti (m)	spaghetti
سبانخ	sabāneχ (m)	spinach
ستيك لحم	steak laḥm (m)	steak
سجق	sogo'' (m)	sausage
سجق	sogo'' (m)	vienna sausage
سخن	soχn	hot
سردين	sardīn (m)	sardine
سعرة حراريّة	so'ra ḥarāriya (f)	calorie
سكّر	sokkar (m)	sugar
سكّينة	sekkīna (f)	knife
سلطة	solṭa (f)	salad
سلمون	salamon (m)	salmon
سلمون أطلسي	salamon aṭlasy (m)	Atlantic salmon
سلمون مرقّط	salamon mera''aṭ (m)	trout
سمسم	semsem (m)	sesame
سمك	samak (m)	fish
سمك الحفش	samak el ḥafʃ (m)	sturgeon
سمك القد	samak el qadd (m)	cod
سمك الكراكي	samak el karāky (m)	pike
سمك الهلبوت	samak el halbūt (m)	halibut
سمك سندر	samak sandar (m)	pike perch
سمك مفلطح	samak mefalṭah (f)	flatfish
سنبلة	sonbola (f)	ear
سي فود	sīfūd (pl)	seafood
شاي	ʃāy (m)	tea
شاي أحمر	ʃāy aḥmar (m)	black tea
شاي أخضر	ʃāy aχḍar (m)	green tea
شبت	ʃabat (m)	dill
شبّوط	ʃabbūṭ (m)	carp
شراب	ʃarāb (m)	aperitif
شريحة	ʃarīḥa (f)	slice
شعير	ʃe'īr (m)	barley
شكولاتة	ʃokolāta (f)	chocolate
شمبانيا	ʃambania (f)	champagne
شمّام	ʃammām (f)	melon
شهيّة	ʃahiya (f)	appetite
شوربة	ʃorba (f)	soup
شوفان	ʃofān (m)	oats
شوكة	ʃawka (f)	fork
شيلم مزروع	ʃelm mazrū' (m)	rye

صفار البيض	ṣafār el beyḍ (m)	egg yolk
صلصة	ṣalṣa (f)	sauce
صيد	ṣeyd (m)	game
طبق	ṭaba' (m)	plate
طبق جانبي	ṭaba' gāneby (m)	side dish
طبق فنجان	ṭaba' fengān (m)	saucer
طعم	ṭa'm (m)	taste, flavor
طعم ما بعد المذاق	ṭa'm ma ba'd el mazāq (m)	aftertaste
طماطم	ṭamāṭem (f)	tomato
عدس	'ads (m)	lentil
عسل	'asal (m)	honey
عشاء	'aʃā' (m)	dinner
عصيدة	'aṣīda (f)	porridge
عصير	'aṣīr (m)	juice
عصير برتقال	'aṣīr bortoqāl (m)	orange juice
عصير طماطم	'aṣīr ṭamāṭem (m)	tomato juice
عصير فريش	'aṣīr freʃ (m)	freshly squeezed juice
عنب	'enab (m)	grape
عنب الأحراج	'enab al aḥrāg (m)	bilberry
عنب الثعلب	'enab el sa'lab (m)	gooseberry
عنب الثور	'enab el sore (m)	cowberry
عنبية حادة الخباء	'enabiya ḥāda el χebā' (m)	cranberry
عيش	'eyʃ (m)	bread
عين الجمل	'eyn gamal (f)	walnut
غداء	ɣada' (m)	lunch
فاصوليا	faṣolya (f)	kidney bean
فاكهة	faχa (f)	fruit
فتاتة	fattāta (f)	crumb
فتّاحة	fattāḥa (f)	bottle opener
فتّاحة	fattāḥa (f)	can opener
فجل	fegl (m)	radish
فجل حار	fegl ḥār (m)	horseradish
فخد خنزير	faχd χanzīr (m)	gammon
فراخ	ferāχ (m)	chicken
فراولة	farawla (f)	strawberry
فراولة برّيّة	farawla barriya (f)	wild strawberry
فرخ	farχ (m)	perch
فستق	fosto' (m)	pistachios
فطر	feṭr (f)	mushroom
فطر أحمر	feṭr aḥmar (m)	orange-cap boletus
فطر أمانيت الطائر	feṭr amanīt el ṭā'er (m)	fly agaric
فطر أمانيت فالوسياني السام	feṭr amanīt falusyāny el sām (m)	death cap
فطر الشانتريل	feṭr el ʃanterel (m)	chanterelle
فطر الغوشنة	feṭr el ɣoʃna (m)	morel
فطر بوليط	feṭr boleṭe (m)	birch bolete
فطر بوليط مأكول	feṭr boleṭe ma'kūl (m)	cep
فطر روسولا	feṭr russula (m)	russula
فطر سام	feṭr sām (m)	poisonous mushroom
فطر صالح للأكل	feṭr ṣāleḥ lel akl (m)	edible mushroom
فطور	foṭūr (m)	breakfast
فطيرة	feṭīra (f)	pie

فلفل	felfel (m)	bell pepper
فلفل أحمر	felfel aḥmar (m)	red pepper
فلفل أسوَد	felfel aswad (m)	black pepper
فنجان	fengān (m)	cup
فودكا	vodka (f)	vodka
فول	fūl (m)	beans
فول الصويا	fūl el ṣoya (m)	soy
فول سوداني	fūl sudāny (m)	peanut
فيتامين	vitamīn (m)	vitamin
فيرموت	vermote (m)	vermouth
قائمة خمور	qā'emet el χomūr (f)	wine list
قائمة طعام	qā'emet el ṭa'ām (f)	menu
قرش	'erʃ (m)	shark
قرع عسلي	qar' 'asaly (m)	pumpkin
قرفة	'erfa (f)	cinnamon
قرموط	'armūṭ (m)	catfish
قرنبيط	'arnabīṭ (m)	cauliflower
قرنفل	'oronfol (m)	cloves
قشرة	'eʃra (f)	peel
قطعة	'eṭ'a (f)	piece
قمح	'amḥ (m)	wheat
قهوة	'ahwa (f)	coffee
قهوة بالحليب	'ahwa bel ḥalīb (f)	coffee with milk
قهوة سادة	'ahwa sāda (f)	black coffee
كابتشينو	kaputʃino (m)	cappuccino
كابوريا	kaboria (m)	crab
كاسة	kāsa (f)	glass
كافيار	kaviar (m)	caviar
كالماري	kalmāry (m)	squid
كانز	kanz	carbonated
كانز	kanz	sparkling
كبدة	kebda (f)	liver
كراوية	karawya (f)	caraway
كرفس	karfas (m)	celery
كرنب	koronb (m)	cabbage
كرنب بروكسل	koronb broksel (m)	Brussels sprouts
كريمة	krīma (f)	cream
كريمة حامضة	kreyma ḥamḍa (f)	sour cream
كريمة زبدة	krīmet zebda (f)	buttercream
كزبرة	kozbora (f)	coriander
كشمش أحمر	keʃmeʃ aḥmar (m)	redcurrant
كشمش أسود	keʃmeʃ aswad (m)	blackcurrant
كمّثرى	komettra (f)	pear
كوبّاية	kobbāya (f)	glass
كورن فليكس	korn fleks (m)	cornflakes
كوسة	kōsa (f)	zucchini
كوكتيل	koktayl (m)	cocktail
كونياك	konyāk (m)	cognac
كيكة	keyka (f)	cake
كيوي	kiwi (m)	kiwi
لبان	lebān (m)	chewing gum
لبن	laban (m)	milk

لحم أرانب	laḥm arāneb (m)	rabbit
لحم الخنزير	laḥm el χanazīr (m)	pork
لحم العجل	laḥm el ʿegl (m)	veal
لحم بقري	laḥm baqary (m)	beef
لحم ضاني	laḥm ḍāny (m)	lamb
لحمة	laḥma (f)	meat
لسان	lesān (m)	tongue
لفت	left (m)	turnip
لوز	loze (m)	almond
ليكيور	liqure (m)	liqueur
ليمون	lymūn (m)	lemon
ليموناتة	limonāta (f)	lemonade
مارجرين	margarīn (m)	margarine
ماكريل	makerel (m)	mackerel
مالح	māleḥ	salty
مانجة	manga (m)	mango
مايونيز	mayonnɛ:z (m)	mayonnaise
مجفّف	mogaffaf	dried
مجمّد	mogammad	frozen
محار	maḥār (m)	oyster
محاصيل الحبوب	maḥaṣīl el ḥubūb (pl)	cereal crops
مخلّل	meχallel	pickled
مدخّن	modakχen	smoked
مربّى	mrabba (m)	jam
مربّى	mrabba (m)	jam
مرقة	maraʾa (m)	clear soup
مرملاد	marmalād (f)	marmalade
مرّ	morr	bitter
مسطردة	mosṭarda (m)	mustard
مسكّر	mesakkar	sweet
مسلوق	maslūʾ	boiled
مشروب غازي	maʃrūb ɣāzy (m)	soft drink
مشروبات كحولية	maʃrūbāt koḥūliya (pl)	liquors
مشمش	meʃmeʃ (f)	apricot
مطبخ	maṭbaχ (m)	cuisine
معجون لحم	maʿgūn laḥm (m)	pâté
معلقة	maʿlaʾa (f)	spoon
معلقة شاي	maʿlaʾet ʃāy (f)	teaspoon
معلّبات	moʿallabāt (pl)	canned food
مقبّلات	moqabbelāt (pl)	appetizer
مقلي	maʾly	fried
مكرونة	makaruna (f)	pasta
ملح	melḥ (m)	salt
ملعقة كبيرة	maʿlaʾa kebīra (f)	soup spoon
من غير كحول	men ɣeyr koḥūl	non-alcoholic
موز	moze (m)	banana
مياه	meyāh (f)	water
ميلك شيك	milk ʃejk (m)	milkshake
ميّة شرب	mayet ʃorb (m)	drinking water
ميّة معدنية	maya maʿdaniya (f)	mineral water
نباتي	nabāty (m)	vegetarian
نباتي	nabāty	vegetarian

نبيذ أبيض	nebīz abyaḍ (m)	white wine
نبيذ أحمر	nebī aḥmar (m)	red wine
نشويّات	naʃawīāt (pl)	carbohydrates
نصيب	naṣīb (m)	portion
نودلز	nūdles (f)	noodles
نيسكافيه	neskafe (m)	instant coffee
هام	hām(m)	ham
هامبورجر	hamburger (m)	hamburger
هامبورجر	hamburger (m)	hamburger
هليون	helione (m)	asparagus
وافلز	waffles (pl)	waffles
وجبة	wagba (f)	course, dish
ورق الغار	wara' el ɣār (m)	bay leaf
وزّة	wezza (f)	goose
وصفة	waṣfa (f)	recipe
ويسكي	wiski (m)	whiskey
ينسون	yansūn (m)	anise
يوسفي	yosfy (m)	mandarin

www.ingramcontent.com/pod-product-compliance
Lightning Source LLC
LaVergne TN
LVHW051731080426
835511LV00018B/2996
* 9 7 8 1 7 8 7 1 6 9 3 1 9 *